W0234751

new interchange

Dorothy E. Zemach

video teacher's guide

CAMBRIDGE
UNIVERSITY PRESS

PUBLISHED BY THE PRESS SYNDICATE OF THE UNIVERSITY OF CAMBRIDGE
The Pitt Building, Trumpington Street, Cambridge, United Kingdom

CAMBRIDGE UNIVERSITY PRESS
The Edinburgh Building, Cambridge CB2 2RU, UK
40 West 20th Street, New York, NY 10011-4211, USA
477 Williamstown Road, Port Melbourne, VIC 3207, Australia
Ruiz de Alarcón 13, 28014 Madrid, Spain
Dock House, The Waterfront, Cape Town 8001, South Africa

http://www.cambridge.org

The publisher has used its best endeavors to ensure that the URLs for Web sites referred to in this book are correct and active at the time of going to press. However, the publisher has no responsibility for the Web sites and can make no guarantee that a site will remain live or that the content is or will remain appropriate.

First published 2002

Printed in the United States of America

Typeface New Century Schoolbook   *System* QuarkXPress®   [AH]

A catalog record for this book is available from the British Library

ISBN 0 521 62844 X Student's Book 3
ISBN 0 521 62843 1 Student's Book 3A
ISBN 0 521 62842 3 Student's Book 3B
ISBN 0 521 62841 5 Workbook 3
ISBN 0 521 62840 7 Workbook 3A
ISBN 0 521 62839 3 Workbook 3B
ISBN 0 521 62838 5 Teacher's Edition 3
ISBN 0 521 62837 7 Teacher's Manual 3
ISBN 0 521 62836 9 Class Audio Cassettes 3
ISBN 0 521 62834 2 Student's Audio Cassette 3A
ISBN 0 521 62832 6 Student's Audio Cassette 3B
ISBN 0 521 62835 0 Class Audio CDs 3
ISBN 0 521 62833 4 Student's Audio CD 3A
ISBN 0 521 62831 8 Student's Audio CD 3B
ISBN 0 521 95019 8 Audio Sampler 1–3
ISBN 0 521 77377 6 Lab Guide 3
ISBN 0 521 77376 8 Lab Cassettes 3

Also available
ISBN 0 521 01094 2 Video 3 (NTSC)
ISBN 0 521 01100 0 Video 3 (PAL)
ISBN 0 521 01097 7 Video 3 (SECAM)
ISBN 0 521 01091 8 Video Activity Book 3
ISBN 0 521 01088 8 Video Teacher's Guide 3
ISBN 0 521 91481 7 Video Sampler Intro–3
ISBN 0 521 46759 4 Placement Test (valid for *New Interchange* and *Interchange*)
ISBN 0 521 80575 9 Teacher-Training Video with Video Manual
Forthcoming
ISBN 0 521 62882 2 *New Interchange / Passages* Placement and Evaluation Package

Art direction, book design, and layout services: Adventure House, NYC

Contents

Plan of Video 3

Introduction

NEW INTERCHANGE

New Interchange is a revision of *Interchange,* one of the world's most successful and popular English courses. *New Interchange* is a multi-level course in English as a second or foreign language for young adults and adults. The course covers the four skills of listening, speaking, reading, and writing, as well as improving pronunciation and building vocabulary. Particular emphasis is placed on listening and speaking. The primary goal of the course is to teach communicative competence, that is, the ability to communicate in English according to the situation, purpose, and roles of the participants. The language used in *New Interchange* is American English; however, the course reflects the fact that English is the major language of international communication and is not limited to any one country, region, or culture. Level Three takes students from the intermediate level up to the high-intermediate level.

Level Three builds on the foundations for accurate and fluent communication already established in Level Two by extending grammatical, lexical, and functional skills. The syllabus covered in Level Three also incorporates a rapid review of language from Level Two, allowing Student's Book 3 to be used with students who have not studied with previous levels.

THE VIDEO COURSE

New Interchange Video 3 is designed to complement the Student's Book or to be used independently as the basis for a short listening and speaking course.

As a complement to the Student's Book, the Video provides a variety of entertaining and instructive live-action sequences. Each video sequence provides further practice related to the topics, language, and vocabulary introduced in the corresponding unit of the Student's Book.

As the basis for a short, free-standing course, the Video serves as an exciting vehicle for introducing and practicing useful conversational language used in everyday situations.

The Video Activity Book contains a wealth of activities that reinforce and extend the content of the Video, whether it is used to supplement the Student's Book or as the basis for an independent course. The Video Teacher's Guide provides thorough support for both situations.

COURSE LENGTH

The Video contains a mix of entertaining, dramatized sequences and authentic documentaries for a total of sixteen sequences. These vary slightly in length, but in general, the sequences are approximately five to eleven minutes each.

The accompanying units in the Video Activity Book are designed for maximum flexibility and provide anywhere from 45 to 90 minutes of classroom activity. Optional activities described in the Video Teacher's Guide may be used to extend the lesson as needed.

MORE ABOUT THE COURSE COMPONENTS

Video

The sixteen video sequences complement Units 1 through 16 of *New Interchange* Student's Book 3. There are seven dramatized sequences and nine documentary sequences. Although linked to the topic of the corresponding Student's Book unit, each dramatized sequence presents a new situation and introduces characters who do not appear in the text. Each documentary sequence is based on authentic, unscripted interviews with people in various situations, and serves to illustrate how language is used by real people in real situations. This element of diversity helps keep students' interest high and also allows the Video to be used effectively as a free-standing course. At the same time, the language used in the video sequences reflects the structures and vocabulary of the Student's Book, which is based on an integrated syllabus that links grammar and communicative functions.

Video Activity Book

The Video Activity Book contains sixteen units that correspond to the video sequences, and is designed to facilitate the effective use of the Video in the classroom. Each unit includes previewing, viewing, and postviewing activities that provide learners with step-by-step support and guidance in understanding and working with the events and language of the sequence. Learners expand their cultural awareness, develop skills and strategies for communicating effectively, and use language creatively.

Video Teacher's Guide

The Video Teacher's Guide contains detailed suggestions for how to use the Video and the Video Activity Book in the classroom, and includes an overview of video teaching techniques, unit-by-unit notes, and a range of optional extension activities. The Video Teacher's Guide also includes answers to the activities in the Video Activity Book and photocopiable transcripts of the video sequences.

■ VIDEO IN THE CLASSROOM

The use of video in the classroom can be an exciting and effective way to teach and learn. As a medium, video both motivates and entertains students. The *New Interchange* Video is a unique resource that does the following:

- Depicts dynamic, natural contexts for language use.
- Presents authentic language as well as cultural information about speakers of English through engaging story lines.
- Enables learners to use visual information to enhance comprehension.
- Focuses on the important cultural dimension of learning a language by actually showing how speakers of the language live and behave.

- Allows learners to observe the gestures, facial expressions, and other aspects of body language that accompany speech.

■ WHAT EACH UNIT OF THE VIDEO ACTIVITY BOOK CONTAINS

Each unit of the Video Activity Book is divided into four sections: *Preview, Watch the Video, Follow-up,* and *Language Close-up*. In general, these four sections include, but are not limited to, the following types of activities:

Preview

Culture The culture previews introduce the topics of the video sequences and provide important background and cultural information. They can be presented in class as reading and discussion activities, or students can read and complete them as homework.

Vocabulary The vocabulary activities introduce and practice the essential vocabulary of the video sequences through a variety of interesting tasks.

Guess the Story/Guess the Facts The Guess the Story (or in some units Guess the Facts) activities allow students to make predictions about characters and their actions by watching the video sequences without the sound or by looking at photos in the Video Activity Book. These schema-building activities help to improve students' comprehension when they watch the sequences with the sound.

Watch the Video

Get the Picture These initial viewing activities help students gain global understanding of the sequences by focusing on gist. Activity types vary from unit to unit, but typically involve watching for key information needed to complete a chart, answer questions, or put events in order.

Watch for Details In these activities, students focus on more detailed meaning by watching and listening for specific information to complete tasks about the story line and the characters or the information in the documentaries.

What's Your Opinion? In these activities, students respond to the sequences by making inferences about the characters' actions and feelings, and by stating their opinions about issues and topics.

Follow-up

Role Play, Interview, and Other Expansion Activities This section includes communicative activities based on the sequences in which students extend and personalize what they have learned.

Language Close-up

What Did They Say? These cloze activities focus on the specific language in the sequences by having students watch and listen in order to fill in missing words in conversations.

Grammar and Functional Activities In these activities, which are titled to reflect the structural and functional focus of a particular unit, students practice, in a meaningful way, the grammatical structures and functions presented in the video sequences.

GUIDELINES FOR TEACHING THE *NEW INTERCHANGE* VIDEO

The Course Philosophy

The philosophy underlying *New Interchange* is that learning a second or foreign language is more meaningful and effective when the language is used for real communication instead of being studied as an end in itself. The *New Interchange* Video and Video Activity Book provide a multi-skills syllabus in which each element in the course is linked.

In the Video Activity Book, for example, the Preview activities build on each other to provide students with relevant background information and key vocabulary that will assist them in better understanding a video sequence. These activities give students the tools for developing essential *top-down processing skills,* the process by which students use background knowledge and relevant information about the situation, context, and topic along with key words and predicting strategies to arrive at comprehension.

The carefully sequenced Watch the Video activities first help students focus on gist and then guide them in identifying important details and language. In addition to assisting students in understanding the sequence, these tasks also prepare them for Follow-up speaking activities, which encourage students to extend and personalize information by voicing their opinions or carrying out communicative tasks.

To conclude students' work with the video sequence, many of the Language Close-up activities focus on developing *bottom-up processing skills,* which require students to decode individual words in a message to derive meaning. The combination of top-down and bottom-up processing skills allows students to understand the general story line of a sequence and the specific language used to tell the story.

Options for the Classroom

The Video Teacher's Guide provides step-by-step instructions for all of the activities in the Video Activity Book. Teachers should not think, however, that there is a limited number of ways to present the material. Most activities can be carried out in a number of ways, and teachers are strongly encouraged to experiment, taking into account the proficiency levels and needs of their students as they plan lessons based on the Video.

Although the procedures for many of the Watch the Video activities state that students should keep their books open while viewing, teachers should feel free to have students try some of these types of activities with their books closed. Likewise, a similar suggestion holds true for other activities that the Video Teacher's Guide suggests be done with books closed – students may benefit from trying certain of these activities with their books open.

The richness of video as a learning medium provides teachers with many options for the classroom. Each lesson in the Video Teacher's Guide describes several classroom-tested activities to extend each sequence and documentary. However, teachers should again note that these suggested activities cover only a few of the many possibilities. Teachers are encouraged to use the Video as a springboard for further classroom activities appropriate to their teaching and learning situations.

General Video Techniques to Try

Once teachers feel comfortable with the basic course procedures, they are encouraged to experiment with other effective – and enjoyable – classroom techniques for presenting and working with the Video. Here are several proven techniques.

Fast-Forward Viewing For activities in which students watch the video sequence with the sound off, play the sequence in fast-forward and have students list all of the things that they can see. For example, for *Sequence 2: Urban artist*, have students watch the sequence in fast-forward and list the kinds of art they see. Nearly all of the activities designed to be completed with the sound off can be done in this manner.

Information Gap Play approximately the first half of a sequence, and then stop the video. Have students work in pairs or groups to predict what is going to happen next. For example, in *Sequence 4: Bigfoot lives!*, stop the video sequence when Cristina says, "Hey, Beth! Come back. I think the mystery of Bigfoot is solved." Ask students, "What do you think Cristina is going to say?" Have students predict the answer, and then play the rest of the sequence so that students can check their predictions.

The procedure for another information-gap activity is as follows: Have half of the students in the class leave the room or turn their backs to the video monitor while the rest of the students view the sequence. Then give the students who have viewed the sequence the task of explaining the basic story line to those who have not seen the sequence. This can be done as a pair, small-group, or class activity.

Act It Out All of the video sequences and documentaries provide an excellent basis for role plays and drama activities. Try this procedure: Select a short scene, and have students watch it several times. Then have pairs or groups act out the scene, staying as close as possible to the actions and

expressions of the characters. Have pairs or groups act out their scenes in front of the class.

Slow Viewing Have students watch a sequence or documentary played in slow motion. As they view, have students call out all of the things they can see people doing or wearing or eating – whatever is appropriate to a particular unit.

What Are They Saying? Have students watch a short segment of a sequence in which two people are talking, but with the sound off. Then have students, working in pairs, use the context to predict what the people might be saying to each other. Have pairs write out sample dialogues, and then share their work with the class.

Freeze-Frame Freeze a frame of a sequence or documentary, and have students call out information about the scene. For example, have students tell about the objects they can see, about what the people are doing, about the time and place – whatever is appropriate to the scene or their learning situation.

▪ HOW TO TEACH A TYPICAL *NEW INTERCHANGE* VIDEO SEQUENCE

The unit-by-unit notes in the Video Teacher's Guide give detailed suggestions for teaching each unit. In addition to these comprehensive notes, here is a set of procedures that can be used to teach any of the units of the *New Interchange* Video.

First, introduce the topic of the unit by asking questions and eliciting information from the students related to the theme of the unit. Then, explain what the students will study (e.g., mention the main topics, functions, and structures), and set the scene. Give students an indication of what they will see in the video sequence. Next, present the activities and tasks using the following guidelines.

Preview

Culture

- Books closed. Introduce the topic by asking questions about it. Use these questions to elicit or present the key vocabulary items and to provide background knowledge on the culture reading. If possible, ask questions that can be answered by reading the text.

- Books open. Have students read the text and check predictions. Teachers may want students to circle no more than three key vocabulary items for which they require definitions.
- Lead the students through the information in the text. Go over any comprehension problems and questions as they arise. Answer any vocabulary questions that still exist.
- Have students complete the task individually or in pairs.
- Have students compare answers with a partner or around the class.

As an alternative, follow this procedure:

- Ask students to read the culture information at home, referring to a dictionary as necessary, and answer the accompanying questions before class.
- Have students compare answers with a partner in class.

In general, teachers should always feel free to provide additional related culture information as appropriate and available.

Vocabulary

- Introduce and model the pronunciation of the words in the activity.
- Have students complete the task in pairs or individually.
- Have students compare answers with a partner or around the class.
- Check students' answers.
- Encourage students to supply additional related vocabulary items where appropriate.

Guess the Story/Guess the Facts

- Ask students to think about the topic of the unit and look at the photos in order to guess what the video sequence is about. Accept all answers at this stage.
- Explain the task, and lead students through the procedure. Answer any questions that arise.
- Play the video sequence with the sound off.
- Have students complete the task individually or in pairs.

- Have students check their predictions and compare answers with a partner or around the class.
- Check students' answers.
- Replay appropriate portions of the video sequence as needed.

Watch the Video

Get the Picture

- Direct students' attention to the task, and read through it with them. Answer vocabulary or procedural questions as they arise.
- Have students work alone and predict answers to questions if they feel they have enough information to do so.
- Remind students that this is a gist activity and that they do not need to try to understand every detail in the sequence. Encourage students to stay focused on the task.
- Play the entire video sequence with the sound on. Replay if necessary.
- Have students complete the task individually or in pairs. When appropriate, have them check the predictions they made in Guess the Story/Guess the Facts as well.
- Have students compare answers with a partner or around the class.
- If time permits, have students check answers while watching the video sequence again.
- Check students' answers.

Watch for Details

- Explain the task. Lead students through the instructions and questions.
- Answer any vocabulary and procedural questions that arise.
- Play the entire video sequence with the sound on. Replay as necessary.
- Have students complete the task individually or in pairs.
- Have students compare answers with a partner or around the class.
- If time permits, have students check their answers while watching the sequence again.
- Check students' answers.

Follow-up

Role Play, Interview, and Other Expansion Activities

Note that since each activity in this section gives students the opportunity to extend and personalize what they have learned in the video sequence and the Video Activity Book, encourage students to use new language to talk about themselves and their ideas as they complete the tasks.

- Explain the task. Lead students through the procedure. Answer vocabulary and procedural questions as they arise.
- Have students complete the task individually, in pairs, or in small groups as noted in the unit instructions.
- Have students compare answers in pairs or in small groups.
- When appropriate, have selected pairs or groups act out the activity for the class.

Language Close-up

What Did They Say?

- Lead students through the task instructions. Answer procedural questions as necessary.
- Have students read the cloze conversation and predict answers when possible.
- Play the appropriate section of the video sequence, and do a spot-check to gauge overall comprehension. Do not supply answers at this stage.
- Play the appropriate section of the video again. Have students compare answers with a partner or around the class.
- Ask if anyone would like to watch the video sequence again. Replay as necessary.
- Go over answers with the class, and discuss any trouble spots.
- If you wish, divide the class in half or in groups, and lead a choral repetition and practice of the cloze conversation.
- When students are comfortable with the dialogue, have them practice it in pairs or small groups, depending on the number of characters required.
- Have selected pairs or groups read or act out the dialogue for the class.

Grammar and Functional Activities

These activities vary from unit to unit, depending on the particular structural and functional focus of a given unit. In general, though, teachers can follow these procedures.

- Present the grammatical structure, and give example sentences from the video script or from students' experiences.
- Lead students through the task, and answer vocabulary and procedural questions as needed.
- Have students complete the task individually or in pairs.
- Have students compare answers with a partner or around the class.
- Check students' answers.
- Review the grammatical structure as appropriate.
- Teachers using *New Interchange* Student's Book 3 should refer students back to the grammar focus in the appropriate unit as necessary.

Optional Activities

The detailed notes for each unit give several optional activities that build on the topic, content, and structural focus of that unit. Teachers are encouraged to select from these suggested activities and use them in class as time permits.

The richness of the visual context leaves additional room for teachers to design and use their own extension activities in class when time is not an issue. Teachers are encouraged to do so.

A Final Note

These suggestions do not represent all of the possibilities for presenting and extending the material in the *New Interchange* Video or the Video Activity Book. Rather, they represent a wide sampling of well-tested activities that teachers are encouraged to use, adapt, modify, and extend to suit the particular needs of their students.

Dream Date

Topic/function: Dating; expressing feelings; describing personalities

Grammar: Clauses containing *it* with adverbial clauses

Summary

The sequence presents a dating game show in which a young woman, Sarah, selects one of three bachelors with whom to have a date. She asks them various questions about their likes and dislikes, their personal qualities, and what they would do in different situations. Bachelor 1 is not ambitious enough, and is only interested in sports. Bachelor 3 is too egotistical, and only thinks about himself. But Bachelor 2 is honest and concerned about other people; he is a good match for Sarah. After she chooses him to be her "dream date," they meet and discover that they knew each other in high school.

 Preview

1 CULTURE

Game shows are popular on TV in North America. Some common types of shows involve answering trivia questions about sports, history, music, popular culture, etc., or guessing how much certain objects cost. Some shows are aired during the day, but most are aired in the evenings. The culture preview in the Video Activity Book provides students with information on dating in North America. If you have students who come from cultures that discourage dating or who are too young to have experience with dating, have them talk about same-sex friendship instead of dates in the following exercises so they can still practice the grammar and vocabulary of the unit.

- Books closed. To introduce the topic, write the following questions on the board:

1) *At what age do you think North Americans start dating?*
2) *How do you think they meet their dates?*
3) *Where do you think they go on dates?*
4) *Who do you think pays for the date?*

- Have students work in pairs, and give them a few minutes to answer the questions. Then ask selected pairs to share their answers with the class.

- Books open. Have students read the culture preview silently to check their predictions and find the correct answers. Then review the answers with the class.

- Put students into small groups to talk about the discussion questions. Tell students to select a secretary in each group to take notes on the discussion.

- Call on each group to present their discussion to the class. If you have students from different countries, write the names of the countries on the board and ask students to record the information under the correct country. If students are from the same country, record differing answers and ask students to explain their answers.

2 VOCABULARY *Personality types*

In this activity, students practice using adjectives to describe personality types used in the sequence by matching descriptions of people with a personality type that describes them.

- Books open. Explain the task, and lead students through the personality types, the descriptions, and the example. Note that in this activity, and in the video sequence, *generous* is used in the sense of *forgiving*.

- **Pair work** Put students into pairs to choose personality types that describe the people.

(procedure continues on next page)

- Have pairs compare answers around the class. Then bring the class together, and have selected students share one or more answers with the class.

Answers
1) egotistical
2) easygoing
3) straightforward
4) ambitious
5) a good conversationalist
6) generous

Optional activities

A *Group work* **Descriptions** Books open. Put students into groups of three or four. Tell them to take turns describing a person they know to illustrate one of the personality types. Model the activity by giving an example of a family member, a neighbor, or a co-worker. Circulate to help and check for accuracy. Call on selected students to share their descriptions with the class. (10 minutes)

B *Class activity* **Role play** Books open. Put students into pairs to write a short role play illustrating one of the personality types. Tell them that they cannot mention the personality word in their role plays. Call on pairs to perform their role plays in front of the class. Tell the class to guess which adjectives were being portrayed. (10 minutes)

---

3 GUESS THE STORY

In this activity, students prepare to watch the sequence by making predictions, based on visual information, about which bachelor Sarah will choose to be her date.

- Books closed. Ask students how important they think personality type is in choosing a person to date. Call on selected students to share their responses with the class.

- Books open. Explain the task, and lead students through the photos and questions.

- Have students work individually to write down how they think Sarah will decide, and which bachelor she will choose.

- Check predictions around the class by tallying them on the board. Ask, "How many of you think Sarah will choose Bachelor 1?", and have students raise their hands. Repeat for Bachelors 2 and 3. Write the number of votes for each bachelor on the board. Tell students that they will find out which bachelor Sarah chooses when they watch the video. (Sarah chooses Bachelor 2.)

- Call on selected students to share reasons for their choices.

 *Watch the video*

4 GET THE PICTURE

In these activities, students watch and listen to the entire sequence in order to check their predictions from Exercise 3, identify questions Sarah asks the bachelors, and identify key personality traits of Sarah and the three bachelors.

A Books open. Read the question, and ask students to raise their hands if they guessed correctly.

B Books open. Explain the task, and read through the questions with the class.

- Books closed. Play the entire sequence with the sound on.

- Have students work alone to check their answers before comparing them with a partner's. Then play the sequence again if necessary.

- Go over the answers with the class by asking selected students to call out answers.

Answers
Sarah asks:
What's your idea of the perfect date?
Tell me something positive and something negative about yourself.
Finish this sentence: "I think it's disgusting when . . ."

C Books open. Explain the task, and lead students through the words in the box. Then give students time to work alone to choose the correct word for each person.

- Have students compare answers in pairs or groups. Then check answers around the class.

Possible answers
1) *Sarah:* excited
2) *Bachelor 1:* easygoing
3) *Bachelor 2:* straightforward
4) *Bachelor 3:* egotistical

Optional activity

Pair work **Additional adjectives** Books closed. Put students into pairs to write some additional words to describe Sarah and the three bachelors. Call on pairs to share their answers, and write new vocabulary on the board. (10 minutes)

Possible answers
> *Sarah:* generous, honest, patient
Bachelor 1: not honest (dishonest), relaxed, sociable
Bachelor 2: honest, direct, modest
Bachelor 3: arrogant, ambitious, opinionated

5 WATCH FOR DETAILS

In this activity, students focus more closely on details in the sequence to correct mistakes in a summary about the bachelors.

- Books open. Explain the task, and read through the summary with the class. Review the sample correction, and make sure students understand that the summary contains other mistakes that they need to correct.

- Ask students to work alone to correct as many errors as they can before watching the sequence. Then have students compare predictions with a partner.

- Books closed. Play the entire sequence with the sound on.

- Books open. Have students work alone to check their predictions and correct the other mistakes in the summary.

- Tell students to compare answers with a partner before you review them with the class.

Answers
Bachelor 1 is **twenty-nine** years old. He's a former college football **star** from Pocatello, Idaho,

who loves playing or watching almost every kind of **sport**. Bachelor 3 is a thirty-year-old **actor** from Los Angeles. Everyone should know his soap opera *My World*. Bachelor 2 comes from Sarah's hometown of Ames, Iowa. In his free time, he enjoys **reading** and surfing the Internet. He and Sarah went to **high school** together.

6 WHO SAID WHAT?

In this activity, students watch and listen more closely to determine who said certain things in the sequence.

- Books open. Explain the task, and lead students through the sentences in the box. Encourage them, working alone or in pairs, to check off the box under the correct bachelor for as many of the sentences as they can before watching the video.

- Play the entire sequence with the sound on. Have students complete the task as they watch and then compare answers with a partner.

- Ask if anyone needs to watch the sequence again, and replay as necessary. Then go over the answers with the class.

Answers
Bachelor 1
1) I'd be too embarrassed to tell you the truth.
7) Well, I guess I'm pretty easygoing.

Bachelor 2
2) It really bothers me when people lie.
4) I'd take you out to a nice dinner.
5) I think I'm a pretty good friend, and people trust me.

Bachelor 3
3) I would take you to my favorite nightclub where everybody knows me.
6) Actually, I'm pretty good at most things I do.

Optional activity

Group work **Making inferences** Books closed. Put students into pairs to write additional statements that each bachelor might make (*not* additional quotes from the sequence). For example, Bachelor 1 might say, "I like to listen to

(procedure continues on next page)

baseball games on the radio." Tell pairs to write at least two or three statements for each bachelor. Circulate to monitor and provide help as needed. Then have each pair join another pair to take turns reading and guessing which bachelor might have said the statements. (10 minutes)

Follow-up

7 ROLE PLAY Let's play Dream Date!

In this extension activity, students further develop their understanding of the sequence by writing additional questions Sarah might ask the bachelors and then role-playing *Dream Date*.

A *Pair work* Books open. Explain the task, and put students into pairs to write more questions for Sarah to ask the bachelors. Write a few examples on the board, such as:

What kind of movies do you like?
What's your idea of the perfect vacation?

■ Circulate to provide help and check for accuracy. When it seems like everyone has finished, ask a few pairs to share their questions with the class.

B *Group work* Books open. Explain the task, and put students into groups of four and have them decide on their roles. If the class has more females than males, you may want to have a male named "Sam" ask three bachelorettes questions.

■ Tell students to act like the video characters they are playing or to create their own characters. In lower-level classes, you may want to have the bachelors read the questions in advance so that they have some time to think of answers. In higher-level classes, the bachelors can respond to the questions on the spot.

■ Have students complete the task. Ask for volunteers to perform their role plays for the class.

Optional activities

A *Group work* **Role play** Books closed. Put students into groups of three to five. Write these role-play variations on the board, and let each group choose one:

Role play 1: Sarah and two to four new bachelors. Each bachelor chooses a personality and occupation.

Role play 2: Sam and two to four bachelorettes. Each bachelorette chooses a personality and occupation.

Give each group time to choose personality traits and occupations, and for Sarah and Jim to write questions to ask. Circulate to help with vocabulary. Have students practice their role plays several times before performing them for the class or another group. (15 minutes)

B *Group work* **Discussion questions** Books closed. Write the following questions on the board:

1) *Are there any dating game shows in your country? If so, what are they like?*
2) *Do you think a game show is a good way to choose a date? Why or why not?*
3) *What are the most important questions to ask a prospective date?*

■ Put students into groups of four or five to discuss the questions. Then ask volunteers to share some of their group's answers. (15 minutes)

Language close-up

8 WHAT DID THEY SAY?

This cloze activity has students focus on specific language used by Sarah and the three bachelors in the sequence.

■ Books open. Have students, working individually or in pairs, read the conversation and fill in as many blanks as they can before watching the video.

■ Play this segment of the video through once (with the picture off, if you prefer) while students work alone to check their predictions and fill in the blanks as they watch and/or listen. Then have students compare answers with a partner.

■ Have students form pairs to compare answers. Then ask, "Does anyone need to watch these conversations again?" Rather than supplying answers, replay the segment as many times as necessary.

■ Check answers around the class by having selected students read one of Sarah's, Bachelor 1's, Bachelor 2's, or Bachelor 3's lines and write the missing words on the board.

■ Model the conversations or, if you wish, do choral or individual repetition. Then put the class into groups of four to practice.

Answers

Sarah: OK. Uh, Bachelor Number 1, finish this sentence: "I **can't stand** it when . . ."

Bachelor 1: I **can't stand** it when people are **talking** while I'm **watching** the football game on TV.

Sarah: OK. Uh, Bachelor Number 3, finish this sentence: "I **think** it's **disgusting** when . . ."

Bachelor 3: I **think** it's **disgusting** when I'm at an expensive **restaurant** and I don't get the **service** I deserve.

Sarah: OK. Bachelor Number 2: "It **really bothers** me when . . ."

Bachelor 2: It **bothers** me when people get **mad** and they get into **arguments** over unimportant things. I just think people should be more **easygoing** and treat each other **better**.

9 *CLAUSES CONTAINING* IT *WITH ADVERBIAL CLAUSES*
Expressing feelings

In this activity, students practice expressing feelings by completing sentences about dating using clauses containing *it* with adverbial clauses – the grammatical focus of the sequence.

A Books open. Explain the task, and lead students through the example and the phrases in the box.

■ Have students work individually to complete the sentences with phrases from the box. Circulate to check for problems, and then have students compare answers with a partner.

■ Check answers around the class, and review the structures as necessary.

Possible answers

1) I can't stand it when my date arrives late.
2) It makes me happy when my date sends me flowers.
3) I like it when my date makes me feel special.
4) It bothers me when my date forgets to call me.
5) It really upsets me when my date lies to me.
6) It embarrasses me when my date talks during a movie.

B *Pair work* Explain the task, and circulate to check for accuracy. Encourage students to ask follow-up questions.

Optional activity

Class activity **Expressing feelings** Books closed. Write the following prompts on the board, and tell students to record them on a piece of paper:

I can't stand it when . . .
It bothers me when . . .
It's embarrassing when . . .

_____

(your own idea)

Have students circulate and ask their classmates to complete the sentences. To practice fluency, tell students that they may make statements that do not have to do with dating. Tell students to record their classmates' responses. Be sure to tell students that they may make up answers and change their responses during the activity. Circulate to provide help as needed. Give students time to interact with as many other students as possible. Then call on selected students to share their recorded responses with the class. You may want to have students vote on which response was the most surprising, the most unusual, and the funniest. (10 minutes)

2 Urban artist

Topic/function: Art in public places;
describing a job

Grammar: Gerunds as subjects and
objects

Summary

In this documentary sequence, we meet artist
José Curbelo, who creates murals in inner-city
neighborhoods in Minneapolis, Minnesota. He
talks about how people have created public art
for thousands of years, for spiritual, political,
and creative reasons. José feels his murals
provide color for a dull urban environment and
give a sense of hope and pride to those who see
and help create them. José first began working
on murals at age thirteen. After high school, he
started his own mural-painting business with
some friends. He attended a special program in
urban art at a college in California and then
returned to Minnesota to create his murals. José
explains that although he may not be highly
paid, he enjoys his job because he feels he is
contributing something positive to the
community, and also because he enjoys working
with the young people who help paint his
murals. We also learn what is involved in
creating a mural in terms of organization,
planning, and funding. First, an appropriate
space for a mural must be found, and then José
and his team draw up plans and ideas. Then
they look for funding, either from business
owners or by applying for grants. If funding is
secured, they buy materials and organize a
schedule for the workers. Finally, José and his
team of young workers paint the mural. We see
examples of José's murals from around the city
of Minneapolis, and we see how they bring color
and creativity to an urban environment.

 *Preview*

1 CULTURE

The culture preview in the Video Activity Book
introduces and builds interest in the topic by
providing background information about
different types of public art and the kinds of
places where it can be found.

■ Books closed. Ask, "What kinds of art can you
see in public places? What kinds of benefits do
you think public art can bring?" Accept all
answers.

■ Books open. Have students silently read the
information in the culture preview. Answer any
vocabulary questions.

■ Have students work in pairs to think of
examples of the types of art mentioned in the
paragraph from the city you are currently in.
Ask, "Does anyone know of any public art near
here?" Ask students who answer "Yes" to
describe where the artwork is and what it looks
like.

■ Put students into groups of three or four to
discuss the questions. Call on selected students
to share some of their group's answers.

Optional activity

Group work **Further discussion questions**
Books closed. Put students into new groups of
three or four, and write these questions on the
board:

1) *Why do you think artists might like to show
their works in public places?*
2) *Who should choose what type of art is shown
in public places?*
3) *Who should pay for public art?*

Tell groups to discuss the questions and assign a
secretary to take notes of their discussion. Then
call on groups to share their group's discussion
with the class. (10 minutes)

2 VOCABULARY Art

In these activities, students practice vocabulary for describing art from the sequence and share their personal opinions about art with their classmates.

A Books closed. Ask the class, "What are some adjectives you can use to describe works of art?" Have students call out words, but do not write them on the board.

■ Books open. Explain the task, and lead students through the words in the box. Then give students time to look at the works of art in the book.

■ Have students work alone to match the vocabulary words to the pictures they think the words describe. Circulate to help out with additional vocabulary if necessary. Do not check answers until students complete part B.

B *Pair work* Books open. Explain the task, and model the example language. Then put students into pairs to take turns sharing their opinions with a partner. Remind pairs that since they are giving personal opinions, they do not need to agree.

■ Check answers around the class by asking questions like, "What words did you use to describe the first picture?", etc. Write new words that students suggest on the board.

Possible answers (from left to right)

political   dull   creative   spiritual
colorful   spiritual   exciting   colorful
(*Note: Creative* could be used as an answer for all four examples.)

3 GUESS THE FACTS

In this activity, students use words from the vocabulary exercise and visual information to make a prediction about the type of art that will be featured in the sequence.

■ Books open. Explain the task, and have students look at the artwork in Exercise 2. Then play the video for one and a half minutes with the sound off (until you see the picture of José as a child).

■ Have students compare predictions with a partner. Encourage them to give reasons for their guesses.

■ Call on selected students to share their predictions with the class. At this point, do not tell students which answer is correct, but explain that the answer will become clear as they continue to work with the sequence. (The sequence is about a muralist.)

Optional activity

Pair work **Describing art** Books closed. Tell students to each make a list of words to describe the works of art they see in the sequence, using the vocabulary words from Exercise 2 and their own ideas. Play the sequence with the sound off for one and a half minutes. Then put students into pairs to compare their answers. Replay the sequence, and pause at each work of art. Call on selected students to share their ideas. (5 minutes)

Possible answers
(*Note:* Students' answers may vary due to personal opinion.)
1) *José Curbelo's murals (shown first):* colorful, creative, exciting
2) *Bull and Vaulter (a Cretan* fresco, *or mural made by mixing paint with wet plaster, from around 2000 b.c.):* colorful, exciting
3) *mosaic of Christ (from the Sancta Sophia church, Istanbul, Turkey; around 1300 a.d.):* spiritual
4) *mural by Diego Rivera (Mexican painter, 1886–1957):* political, colorful, exciting

 **Watch the video**

4 GET THE PICTURE

In these activities, students watch and listen in order to put the steps of creating a mural in the proper order. Then students personalize the information by talking about which of the steps they would enjoy doing most.

(procedure continues on next page)

A Books open. Explain the task, and lead students through the list of steps. Encourage students to predict as many answers as they can before watching the sequence, and then have students compare predictions with a partner.

■ Play the entire sequence with the sound on so that students can check and revise their predictions.

■ Find out if anyone needs to watch the sequence again, and replay as needed.

■ Ask students to compare answers with a partner, and then check answers around the class.

Answers
1) look for a wall
2) plan and draw ideas
3) find funding
4) buy materials
5) set a schedule for the workers
6) paint the mural

B *Pair work* Explain the task, and then put students into pairs to take turns discussing the steps they would or would not enjoy doing.

■ Call on volunteers to share their choices with the class. Encourage students to give reasons for their choices.

5 WATCH FOR DETAILS

In this activity, students focus more closely on the sequence in order to decide whether details about it are true or false.

A Books open. Explain the task, and lead students through the list of statements.

■ Have students predict whether each statement is true or false and then compare predictions with a partner before viewing.

■ Play the entire sequence with the sound on. Have students check off their answers in the chart as they watch and listen.

■ Ask if anyone needs to view the sequence again, and replay as necessary. Then have students compare answers with a partner.

■ Have students, working individually or in pairs, correct the false statements. If necessary, replay the sequence, and then check answers around the class.

Answers
1) True
2) False (People have expressed themselves in a public way for hundreds of thousands of years.)
3) True
4) True
5) False (He attended a special program in urban art at a college in California.)
6) False (Sometimes José has to find his own funding.)
7) False (José's workers are between fourteen and eighteen years old; José is twenty-two.)
8) False (He works in Minneapolis, Minnesota, now.)

B *Pair work* Books open. Explain the task, and replay the sequence. Then give students a few minutes to write their statements. Circulate to provide help if necessary.

■ Put students into pairs to take turns reading their statements to a partner. The partners decide if the statements are true or false. Encourage students to correct false statements that they identify.

Optional activity

Pair work **More true/false statements**
Books open or closed. Have students work in pairs to write three statements about the sequence: one true and two false. Have each pair exchange statements with another pair. Students should then watch the sequence again and mark each statement as true or false. To complete the task, have students correct the false statements and then check their answers with the pair that wrote the statements. Ask selected students to read one of their statements to the class, and have the class answer "True" or "False." (10 minutes)

6 WHAT'S YOUR OPINION?

In these activities, students decide which statements about job preferences describe José Curbelo, and then talk about their own job preferences. Finally, they match a list of jobs with job preference descriptions.

A Books open. Explain the task, and read the phrases with the class. Then have students check the phrases that describe what José prefers in a work situation.

▪ Check answers around the class by asking individual students to share an answer with the class. Encourage students to give reasons or evidence from the sequence to support their answers.

Answers
1) working with people
2) doing interesting work
3) doing something different every day
4) working outside
5) being the boss

B *Pair work* Books open. Explain the task, and read the example. Then put students into pairs to take turns asking and answering the questions. When students have finished, call on selected students to tell the class about their partners (e.g., "Maria would prefer working with people.").

C *Pair work* Explain the task, and read the jobs in the box and the example language. Then put students into new pairs to make sentences to describe the jobs in the box.

▪ For each job, call on selected students to share their answers. Finally, take a class poll to find out the most popular and the least popular job.

Optional activity

***Pair and group work* Attitudes and jobs**
Books closed. Write the following prompts on the board:

*doing creative work / doing routine work
working with people / working with machines
having a lot of responsibility / having an
    easy job
taking business trips / staying in the
    same place*

Put students into pairs to take turns asking and answering questions like, "Would you prefer doing creative work or doing routine work?" Then put pairs together. Have students take turns telling their group what kind of job they would recommend for their partner and why (e.g., "I think Ayaka should be an actress because she would prefer doing creative work and being famous."). (10 minutes)

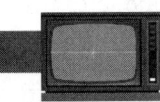 *Follow-up*

7 BEAUTIFYING YOUR AREA

In this communicative activity, students think about how their own communities could be beautified with public art and discuss ways to accomplish this.

A *Pair work* Books open. Explain the task, and go over the chart. Then put students into pairs to complete the chart. Circulate to help out with vocabulary as necessary. Encourage students to provide as many details as they can.

B *Group work* Books open. Explain the task, and read the example language. Have each pair join another pair, and give them a few minutes to share their suggestions.

▪ Call on selected students from each group to present their group's suggestions to the class.

Optional activity

***Pair work* Beautifying your classroom**
Books closed. Put students into pairs, and divide the pairs into two groups. Have half of the pairs do *Task 1* and the other half do *Task 2*.

Task 1: You have an unlimited budget. Design a beautiful room for our class. What kinds of art will be in it?

Task 2: Think of as many ways as you can to beautify our classroom. What kinds of art could we add?

Call on *Task 1* pairs to present their ideas to the class. Then say, "Unfortunately, we didn't get the funding for these projects. However, we do have enough money to fix up the classroom we already have." Then have *Task 2* pairs present their ideas to the class. (15 minutes)

 **Language close-up**

8 WHAT DID HE SAY?

This cloze activity has students focus on specific language used by José Curbelo to explain why he enjoys painting murals.

■ Books open. Have students work alone to fill in as many blanks as they can before watching the sequence. Then have students compare predictions in pairs.

■ Play this segment of the sequence through once, and have students work alone to check their predictions and fill in the blanks as they watch.

■ Have students compare answers with a partner. Then ask if anyone needs to watch the video again, and replay as necessary.

■ Play the segment once more as a final check so that students can check their answers.

■ Check answers around the class by asking students to take turns reading sentences, or by reading the answers yourself.

Answers

José: I love **working** with **people**. I love **doing** my own thing, I love **writing** my own paycheck, and I like to be **involved** in the life of the . . . **the community**. **Working** on murals, you're at one **place** – at one street corner – for twelve, fourteen **hours** a day, and you see **everything** that goes on. In my **opinion**, the murals are **necessary** to the life of a community, **because** ever since way back when – **hundreds** of thousands of years ago – people have **expressed** themselves in a **public** way. Whether for **spiritual** reasons or for **political** reasons, or just to be **creative**, people have expressed themselves on **walls**, and I wouldn't be **doing** what I'm doing now if . . . you know, **people** didn't write on **caves** . . . you know, thousands of years ago or write on **subway** trains in the seventies.

Optional activity

Pair work **Interview** Books open. Put students into pairs. Explain that one student is a reporter, and the other is José Curbelo. The reporter will interview José Curbelo. Have students reread José's commentary in Exercise 8 together and write some questions for the reporter (e.g, *What do you like about your job? How many hours a day do you work on a mural? Why are murals necessary to the life of a community?*). Then have the reporter interview José. Have volunteer pairs present their interviews to the class. (10 minutes)

9 GERUNDS AS SUBJECTS AND OBJECTS Describing a job

In these activities, students practice both the functional and the grammatical focus of the unit by using subject and object gerunds to describe jobs.

A Books open. Explain the task, and read through the gerund forms in the box. Have students work alone to complete the sentences. Then have students compare answers with a partner.

■ Check answers around the class by having selected students read aloud one sentence at a time.

■ Ask the class what job they think is being described. Accept any answers that students can reasonably defend by using information from the sentences.

Answers
1) working with children
2) Staying in shape
3) working on weekends
4) organizing the game schedule
5) improving their skills
6) Encouraging

Job described: Children's athletic coach (e.g., soccer, baseball, etc.).

B *Pair work* Books open or closed. Explain the task, and have students work individually to choose a job and think of the duties of that job.

■ Put students into pairs to take turns describing their job duties to their partners, who try to guess the job.

■ If time permits, have students change partners and repeat the exercise.

3 Kid sister

Topic/function: Baby-sitting; asking favors

Grammar: Indirect requests

Summary

In this sequence, Abby is called out of town overnight on business. However, she's supposed to baby-sit her 13-year-old sister, Kathy, at the same time. She calls her friend Renee to ask for help, and Renee agrees to take care of Kathy for the night. When Kathy arrives, Renee is worried about getting along with her – Kathy looks wild and uncommunicative. Kathy keeps her headphones for her portable CD player on all the time with loud music playing. She asks to watch television, but turns the volume up too loud, and Renee has to ask her to turn it down. She asks to use the phone and won't hang up when Renee tells her it's time for dinner. She asks to use Renee's laptop computer, but Renee explains that she's working on it. She knocks over Renee's stack of CDs, which Renee cleans up while Kathy finally eats her dinner. It seems as though the two have nothing in common until Kathy falls asleep reading Renee's copy of a *Harry Potter* novel. In the morning, she and Renee talk excitedly about how much they both like the book. When Abby arrives to pick Kathy up, she finds the two new friends deep in conversation.

Preview

1 CULTURE

In North America, baby-sitting is a common way for teens to make money. Typically, teens and college students make from $5 to $10 an hour to watch babies or young children whose parents are away for a few hours. Organizations such as the Red Cross and the YMCA offer classes on baby-sitting that teach young adults how to care for children safely and effectively. In some cultures, baby-sitting may not be common because couples don't go out at night very often, parents don't trust the care of their children to teenagers, or parents live with or close to relatives who could watch their children if necessary. The culture preview in the Video Activity Book gives students information about the customs of baby-sitting in North America. (*Note: Harry Potter* is a children's series that is very popular with teens and adults as well. It features the adventures of a young boy and his friends who attend a school for wizards and witches.)

■ Books closed. Tell students, "We're going to read a list of advice for baby-sitters. What advice do you think will be on the list?" Give an example, and ask students to work in pairs or small groups to list at least three pieces of advice that they think will be on the list.

■ Circulate to help with vocabulary and to keep students on task. After a few minutes, bring the class back together and have a spokesperson from each group share the group's list with the class. Write students' ideas on the board.

■ Books open. Have students read the culture information silently to check their predictions. Then ask selected students to read aloud advice in the text that hasn't been mentioned yet.

■ Put students into pairs or small groups to answer the questions as you circulate.

■ When talk begins to die down, bring the class back together and have selected students share their answers with the class. Write the suggestions on the board.

2 VOCABULARY *Requests and responses*

This activity introduces some of the language of requests and responses that students will hear in the video. Students match requests with their responses and then practice them with a partner.

Pair work Books open. Explain the task, and go over the example. Then put students into pairs to match the requests with the responses.

■ Have pairs compare answers with others. Go over the answers with the class by asking a student to read a request and having his or her partner respond. Ask for a volunteer to record the requests and responses on the board.

Answers

1) d   No, sorry. I'm expecting a call.
2) a   No, go ahead. The keys are on the table.
3) f   Sure. Or I can pick her up.
4) b   OK. I'll tell her.
5) c   Sure. What can I do?
6) e   Not at all. I'd be happy to have her.

Tell students to practice the requests and responses.

Optional activity

Pair work **Making requests** Books closed. Ask students to each write a list of at least three requests they might make in a typical week. Write these examples on the board:

Is it all right if I borrow your textbook?
Would you mind lending me some money for a
   cup of coffee?
Could you tell me the time?

Then put students into pairs to take turns making each request twice to a partner, who first grants and then denies the request. Encourage students to give reasons for their refusals, if possible. Write these examples on the board:

I'm sorry, I left my book at home too.
I'm afraid I don't have any money.
Sorry, my watch is broken.

Remind students to say "I'm afraid" or "I'm sorry" and to sound sincere when apologizing. Finally, have pairs memorize one or two of their dialogues to present to the class. (15 minutes)

3 GUESS THE STORY

In this activity, students use visual information to predict a general question about the people in the sequence.

■ Books open. Have students work alone to write their predictions. Then have them compare predictions with a partner.

■ Check predictions around the class. Accept all answers, but encourage students to explain how they made their predictions. Be sure not to confirm answers at this point. Instead, tell students they will find out what the women were talking about when they watch the entire sequence. (One woman is asking her friend the favor of baby-sitting her younger sister.)

Optional activity

Class activity **Making predictions** Books closed. Write the title of the unit, "Kid sister," on the board. Then play the video with the sound off for two minutes (until Abby leaves Renee's apartment). Ask students these questions:

1) What do you think this story is going to be about?
2) Why do you think the girl is going to the woman's apartment?

Accept any answers. Then play the video with the sound off for another two minutes (until Renee takes the pizza from the freezer), and ask these questions:

1) How are the girl and the woman getting along?
2) What problems do you think they're having?
3) What do you think will happen next?

Accept any answers, but encourage students to explain their predictions. (10 minutes)

 **Watch the video**

4 GET THE PICTURE

In these activities, students watch and listen to the entire sequence to put the situations in order and then match requests with the pictures that the requests describe.

■ Books open. Explain the task, and give students time to look at the pictures. Then have students work individually or in pairs to guess the order of the pictures before watching the sequence.

(procedure continues on next page)

■ Play the entire sequence through with the sound on. Have students check their predictions and compare answers with a partner.

■ If necessary, play the sequence again before going over the answers.

Answers (from left to right)

4	3	1
2	5	6

Tell students to work individually to match the requests with the pictures.

■ Check answers by holding up the book, pointing to a picture, and asking students to call out the correct request.

Answers (from left to right)

Would you mind my using it?

Would you turn the volume down?

Is it OK if I drop her off on my way to the airport?

Would you mind if I listened to some of them?

Is it all right if I take a shower?

Is it all right if I use your phone to call one of my friends?

Optional activities

A *Class activity* **Responses to requests**
Books closed. Play the sequence again, and have students indicate whether the requests in Exercise 4 were granted or denied. Tell students to call out the answers. If a request is denied, stop the video and tell students to call out the reason. (5 minutes)

Answers
All requests are granted except number 4, "Would you mind my using it?", which Renee turns down because she is using the laptop for work.

B *Pair work* **Handling problems** Books closed. Put students into pairs to watch the sequence again. Tell pairs to make a list of the problems in the sequence (e.g., Abby needs to go out of town when she's supposed to be baby-sitting her sister, Kathy.). Then have each pair brainstorm possible solutions, other than those in the sequence, to each problem. Have pairs share their favorite solutions with the class. (15 minutes)

5 MAKING INFERENCES

In this activity, students watch and listen more closely in order to make inferences – reach conclusions even when the information is not explicitly stated – about what happens in the sequence.

■ Books open. Explain the task, and tell students that making an inference is like making a good guess based on what you know. Use the first statement as an example, if necessary. Read the statement and then say, "Is this true or false? How do we know?" (Abby's boss had just called her to ask her to go out of town that afternoon. Also, when Abby dropped her sister off, she told Renee, "I have to run.")

■ Read the statements with the class, and encourage them to predict the answers before they watch the sequence.

■ Play the sequence with the sound on. Have students work alone to check their predictions and mark *True* or *False* as they watch.

■ Play the sequence several times if necessary. Then have students compare answers with a partner.

■ Check answers around the class by asking individual students to share an answer with the class. Encourage students to give reasons or evidence from the sequence to support their answers.

■ Alternatively, check answers by playing the video with the sound on and in slow motion, if possible. Have students call out "Stop" when they hear or see evidence to support an answer. A volunteer then tells the class what the evidence is (e.g., "Renee answers, 'No, I wouldn't mind at all' when Abby asks her to baby-sit."). Continue like this until you have gone over all the statements.

Answers

1)	True	5)	False
2)	False	6)	False
3)	True	7)	True
4)	False		

6 WHO SAID WHAT?

In this activity, students watch and listen more closely to determine who said certain things in the sequence.

■ Books open. Explain the task, and then lead students through the sentences in the box. Before watching the video, have students work alone or in pairs to check off the box under the correct name for as many of the sentences as they can.

■ Play the entire sequence with the sound on. Have students complete the task as they watch and then compare answers with a partner.

■ Ask if anyone needs to watch the sequence again, and replay as necessary. Then go over the answers with the class.

Answers
Abby
1) She's going through a stage.
6) Actually, I'm late.

Renee
3) Is there anything I can get for you?
5) You were reading *Harry Potter*?

Kathy
2) Wow, you've got a lot of CDs!
4) Do you have anything to eat around here?

Optional activity

Pair work **Guessing what characters might say** Books closed. Put students into pairs to think of at least two more sentences or requests for each of the three characters. Explain that these sentences should be things the characters *might* say rather than something they actually said in the sequence. Then have each pair join another pair to take turns sharing their new sentences and guessing the identity of the speakers. (10 minutes)

Follow-up

7 ROLE PLAY Can you help me out?

In this extension activity, students have the chance to be creative by imagining that they are either having a big party over the weekend or moving to a new apartment and must request help from a friend.

A ***Pair work*** Books open. Explain the task, put students into pairs, and then model the example conversation below the box. Point out that Student A must make two requests of Student B. Tell Student B that the requests can be granted or denied.

■ Give Student A time to write two requests while Student B reviews ways of responding to requests by jotting down possible responses. Circulate to help out with vocabulary and to prompt students if they have difficulty thinking of requests or responses.

■ Have students begin the activity. To encourage more than yes-or-no responses, write the following comments on the board:

No problem.
I'd be happy to help.
I'm sorry, but I'm busy that day.

■ Give pairs time to practice their role plays several times, and then call on pairs to present their role plays to the class.

B ***Pair work*** Repeat the procedure in part A above.

Optional activity

Pair work **Role plays** Books closed. Put students into new pairs. Have each student choose one of the following situations: planning a picnic, studying together, taking a class trip, or their own idea. Tell each student to write new requests for the situation and then to ask their partner for help. Circulate to check for accuracy and to help with vocabulary. Give students time to practice their role plays. Then call on pairs to present their role plays to the class. (10 minutes)

Language close-up

8 WHAT DID THEY SAY?

This cloze activity has students watch and listen to complete the opening conversation between Abby and Renee.

■ Books open. Have students, working individually or in pairs, fill in as many blanks as they can before watching the video.

■ Play this segment of the sequence as many times as necessary while students work alone to check their predictions and fill in the blanks as they watch.

■ Have students compare answers with a partner. Then replay the sequence so students can check their answers. Replay the sequence as many times as necessary.

■ Check answers around the class, and then play the segment again as a final check.

■ Model the conversation or, if you wish, lead a choral or individual repetition of it to prepare for pair work. Then put students into pairs to practice the conversation.

Answers

Abby: Renee? I am so **glad** you're there. I was **wondering** if you could help me out.

Renee: **What's up**?

Abby: I **need** to ask a big **favor**. My **boss** just called, and he wants me to go out of town **this afternoon** to meet with a client.

Renee: **Great!** You wanted to **work** with more clients.

Abby: Yeah. But the problem is my **parents** are out of town and my little sister is **staying** with me for the **weekend**.

Renee: Hmm. That *is* a **problem**.

Abby: Yeah, that's why I'm **calling**. **Would you mind** if she stayed with you? It would only be for **tonight**. I'll pick her up **tomorrow morning** by ten o'clock.

Renee: No, I **wouldn't mind** at all. But **could** you **ask** her to **bring** something to entertain herself while I **work** on my **report**?

Abby: Sure, **no problem**.

9 INDIRECT REQUESTS
Asking favors

These activities give students practice in both the functional and the grammatical focus of the unit by having them use indirect requests to ask favors.

A Books open. Explain the task, and read the expressions in the box. Then have students work alone to complete Abby and Renee's phone conversation.

■ Have students compare answers with a partner. Then call on volunteers to take turns reading Abby and Renee's lines in the phone conversation.

Answers

Abby: Would you mind taking in the mail every day?

Abby: Great. And could you feed the fish?

Abby: And let's see. I was wondering if you could take phone messages?

Abby: Great. Oh, and I was wondering if you'd mind walking the dog?

Abby: Only three times a day. Anyway, one more thing. Is it OK if Kathy spends the weekend?

■ If time permits, put students into pairs to practice the conversation. Have them take turns as Abby and Renee.

B Pair work Books open. Explain the task, and put students into pairs. Tell students to brainstorm several requests and to jot them down on a separate piece of paper. Circulate to check grammar and help with vocabulary.

■ Have students take turns asking each other favors. If possible, encourage students to role-play a phone call similar to the one in part A.

■ Call on students to share their requests with the class.

4 Bigfoot lives!

Topic/function: Mysterious and unusual creatures; telling a story in the past

Grammar: Past tense verbs – past continuous, simple past, and past perfect

Summary

In this sequence, Amy, Beth, and Cristina are camping in the woods. Amy comes back from the bathhouse to tell her two friends that she's been told the story of a "Bigfoot sighting" – a couple saw a large, hairy creature near their campsite. Cristina doesn't believe the story, but Beth is nervous. As Beth walks to the bathhouse, she hears a growling sound and then sees a mysterious, shaggy creature in the woods. She screams and runs back to the campsite alone. Cristina goes with her to look for the creature. When Beth comes back to the campsite, Amy shows her some Bigfoot tracks. Beth becomes frightened and decides to go home, but Cristina returns and announces that there is no Bigfoot. She's found a bearskin and a tape recorder that makes growling sounds in the woods. She accuses Amy of playing a joke, and Amy admits it's true. Beth forgives her but makes her promise not to play any more tricks. But as the three girls settle around the campfire, they hear a mysterious growl.

 **Preview**

1 CULTURE

The sequence shows Amy telling a scary story on a camping trip. Telling stories around the campfire about ghosts or mysterious creatures is a popular activity for teens and young adults. The culture preview in the Video Activity Book gives students some information about storytelling in North America.

■ Books closed. To introduce the topic, ask the class the following questions and have students respond by raising their hands:

1) What are some situations when people tell stories to each other?
2) When do people tell scary stories?
3) Why do you think people tell scary stories?

■ Have those who raised their hands share their responses with the class. Accept all answers and, if you wish, record them on the board.

■ Books open. Have students read the information in the culture preview silently. Answer any vocabulary questions.

■ Put students into groups of three or four to discuss the questions.

Optional activity

Group work **Storytelling** Books closed. Write these questions on the board:

1) What makes a story scary?
2) What makes a story seem believable?
3) What makes a person a good storyteller?

■ Then put students into small groups to discuss the questions. Call on groups to share their discussions with the class. (15 minutes)

2 VOCABULARY Descriptions

In this activity, students practice distinguishing words with similar meanings used in the sequence by matching them with a corresponding picture.

■ Books open. Explain the task. Have students look at each set of pictures. Then read through the choices for each set of pictures. Have students repeat after you to practice pronunciation.

■ Have students work individually to match the vocabulary words to the pictures, and then have them compare answers with a partner. Check the answers as a class.

(see next page for answers)

Answers

1) an incredible story, a ridiculous story
2) a mysterious situation, a scary situation
3) a growl, a howl
4) an encounter, a sighting

Optional activity

Group work **Vocabulary extension** Books open. Put students into pairs, and have them write sentences that either suggest vocabulary words from Exercise 2 (e.g., *I met my friend coming home from school the other day.* [encounter]) or that use vocabulary words from Exercise 2 (e.g., *There hasn't been a Bigfoot sighting in my neighborhood.*). Write the examples of each type of sentence on the board. When pairs have finished their sentences, have them join another pair to take turns reading their sentences saying "blank" in place of the word if they're using it in the sentence. The other pair tries to guess which word is being suggested. (15 minutes)

Possible sentences

1) *encounter:* I met my friend coming home from school the other day.
   sighting: I saw a strange animal in the yard, but I don't think it saw me.
2) *mysterious:* I can't explain that at all! It's very _____ .
   scary: Whenever I see _____ movies, I have trouble falling asleep because I'm frightened.
3) *growl:* The dog _____ at me because it didn't know me.
   howl: That dog _____ at the moon.
4) *ridiculous:* That's the funniest story I've ever heard! It's completely _____ .
   incredible: That's an _____ story. I find it hard to believe.

---

3 GUESS THE STORY

In this activity, students prepare to watch the sequence by making predictions, based on visual information, about who believes the Bigfoot story.

■ Books closed. Ask students if they have ever heard of the creature Bigfoot. If any say "Yes," ask what they know about it. Then read this passage to the class (the passage does not appear in the Video Activity Book).

"First named in the 1950s, 'Bigfoot,' or 'Sasquatch,' as it is known in Canada, is thought by some to be a large, hairy apelike creature who lives in the woods of North America. Such a creature has never been captured alive, nor has the body of a dead one ever been found. But there are thousands of reports each year from people who claim to have seen a Bigfoot or some of its tracks. Scientists, naturalists, and others still argue about whether creatures like Bigfoot really exist, or whether they are just the result of mistakes or people's imaginations."

■ Read the passage again, if necessary, and ask students if they think a creature such as this could exist. Call on volunteers to offer reasons for their opinions. Then write three columns on the board labeled: Definitely, Maybe, and Absolutely Not. Point to each column, and ask students to raise their hands to vote on whether Bigfoot definitely exists, maybe exists, or absolutely does not exist.

■ Books open. Explain the task, and make sure students understand that more than one woman could believe the story.

■ Play the first two and a half minutes with the sound off (until Beth goes to the bathhouse and the other two girls sit by the fire) as students watch and guess who believes the story.

■ Have students compare answers with a partner. Then ask selected students to share their answers with the class. Accept all answers at this point, and be sure not to give away the actual answer. Explain that they will find out the answer in the next activity. (The answers are given in Exercise 4 of this book.)

 *Watch the video*

4 GET THE PICTURE

In this activity, students check the accuracy of their predictions in Exercise 3 and then focus on Amy, Beth, and Cristina to decide whether statements about the three women are true or false.

A Books open. Explain the task, and have students look back at the predictions they made in Exercise 3.

▪ Play the sequence with the sound on, and have students check and correct their predictions while viewing.

▪ Have students compare answers with a partner. Then ask if anyone needs to watch the sequence again, and replay as necessary.

▪ Go over the answers with the class.

Answers
Amy doesn't believe the story.
Beth believes the story.
Cristina doesn't believe the story.

B Books open. Explain the task, and read through the statements with the class. Encourage students to predict whether each statement is true or false before they view.

▪ Play the entire sequence with the sound on. Have students work alone to check their predictions and mark each statement as true or false as they watch and listen.

▪ Ask students to compare their answers with others as you circulate to check for accuracy. Before going over the answers with the class, replay the sequence as needed.

▪ Have students work in pairs to correct the false statements. If necessary, replay the sequence. Then check answers around the class.

Answers
1) True
2) False (Beth sees Amy dressed as Bigfoot on her way to the bathhouse.)
3) False (Amy tells the others that she heard a story about a Bigfoot encounter.)
4) True

Optional activities

A *Group work* **Storytelling follow-up**
Books closed. If students did the Exercise 1 Optional activity, have them say whether they thought Amy's story was scary and/or believable, and whether they thought Amy was a good storyteller, according to the criteria they discussed before watching the sequence. (10 minutes)

B *Pair work* **More true/false questions**
Books open or closed. Have students work in pairs to write three more true/false statements like the ones in Exercise 4.

▪ Put two or three pairs together to share their statements. Have students predict which statements are true and false before watching the sequence again.

▪ Play the sequence again, and have pairs correct each other's answers. (10 minutes)

---

5 WATCH FOR DETAILS

In this activity, students watch and listen more closely in order to complete more detailed sentences about the story.

▪ Books open. Explain the task, and lead students through the example.

▪ Have students, working individually or in pairs, fill in as many blanks as they can at this point.

▪ Play the entire sequence with the sound on. Have students work alone to check their predictions and fill in the blanks as they watch.

▪ Ask students to compare answers with a partner or around the class. Then ask if anyone needs to watch the sequence again to complete the task. Replay the video as needed before checking answers with the class.

Answers
1) Canada
2) shower and brush her teeth
3) light
4) flashlight and towel
5) an animal – a *small* animal
6) footprints (tracks)
7) a costume (bearskin) and a tape recorder

6 MAKING INFERENCES

In this activity, students watch the women's facial expressions and body language more closely in order to make inferences about their feelings. Then they personalize the activity by discussing times when they have felt the same emotions as the women.

A Books open. Explain the task, and make sure that students understand the meaning of each word in the box. Give students time to look at the pictures, and encourage students to predict as many answers as they can at this point.

▪ Play the entire video with the sound on. Tell students to complete the task as they watch and then compare answers with a partner. Explain that the characters don't always say what they feel, but their facial expressions usually give away their true feelings.

▪ Check answers around the class, and replay the sequence as needed.

Answers (from left to right)

nervous	disbelieving	surprised
apologetic	angry	excited

B *Pair work* Books open. Explain the task, and read the example language. Then put students into pairs to take turns telling each other about times when they have felt the emotions described in part A.

Optional activity

Class activity or group work **Emotions charades** Books closed. Put students into groups of four or five. Write these cues on the board:

hearing a strange sound
watching a movie
hearing some news over the telephone
opening a letter
seeing someone you know across the street
talking to your friend

Explain to students that they are going to take turns making a facial expression in response to each of these events. Group members must guess which emotion is being portrayed. If time permits, elicit more cues from students and write them on the board. Continue the activity in groups. (10 minutes)

 *Follow-up*

7 DO YOU BELIEVE THESE STORIES?

This extension activity gives students the opportunity to discuss the Loch Ness Monster, Alien Big Cats, and other unusual creatures.

▪ Books open. Explain the task, and call on students to read the paragraphs aloud, or give students time to read them silently. Go over any new vocabulary, and answer any questions students may have.

▪ *Group work* Point out the example language. Then put students into groups to discuss each creature. Tell groups to assign a secretary to take notes during the group's discussion.

▪ Call on the group secretaries to present their group's discussion to the class.

Optional activities

A *Group work* **Mysterious creatures** Books closed. Put students into groups of three or four, and tell them they will create a story about a mysterious creature they have heard of, or one they make up. If possible, give each group a large piece of paper and some colored markers and encourage them to draw a picture of their animal in its habitat. Circulate to provide help and prompt groups who are stuck for ideas (e.g., "Could your creature live in the water/underground/in outer space? Does it eat plants or animals? How big is it?"). When groups have finished, have them take turns telling the class about their creature. If they have drawn a picture of the creature, have them hold it up as they speak. Encourage other groups to ask questions for additional information. (15 minutes)

B *Group work* **Discussion questions** Books closed. Write these questions on the board:

1) *What kind of evidence would prove or disprove the existence of Bigfoot, the Loch Ness Monster, and Alien Big Cats?*
2) *Why do you think people haven't been able to prove or disprove their existence yet?*
3) *Why are people interested in hearing about creatures like these?*

Put students into groups of four or five to discuss the questions. When groups have finished their discussions, ask for volunteers to each share some of their group's answers with the class. (15 minutes)

Language close-up

8 WHAT DID THEY SAY?

This cloze activity has students focus on specific language used by Cristina and Beth to confront Amy with evidence of her trick.

■ Books open. Have students read through the conversation and, working individually or in pairs, fill in as many blanks as they can before watching.

■ Play this segment of the sequence as many times as necessary. Have students work alone to check their predictions and fill in the blanks as they watch.

■ Have students compare answers with a partner and then watch this segment once more as a final check.

■ Model the conversation or, if you wish, lead a choral or individual repetition of it. Then put students into groups of three to practice. Have groups practice the conversation three times so that each student has a chance to play each of the three characters.

Answers

Amy: You don't think *I* did it!
Cristina: I do. First, **before** you told us **about** Bigfoot, you **had already left** a bearskin and tape recorder **hidden** in the woods. Then, when Beth **left** to take a shower, you **went** to get some **sticks** to toast the marshmallows. You were **gone** when Beth had her **encounter** with Bigfoot.
Amy: That was **just** a coincidence!
Cristina: Was it? You **didn't come** with us when Beth and I went to get her **flashlight** and things. After we left, you had **plenty** of time to reset the

recorder and to make the **footprints** before we **returned**.
Beth: Aha! Busted!
Amy: You're **pretty** good, Cristina. I **didn't think** I'd get **caught**.

9 PAST TENSE VERBS

Telling a story

In these activities, students practice both the grammatical focus and the functional focus of the unit by using three forms of past tense verbs (past perfect, past continuous, and simple past) to relate stories about sightings or encounters with mysterious creatures.

A Books closed. To review past tense verbs, ask students to call out common situations in which English speakers use the past perfect (to describe an action that occurs before another past action), the past continuous (to describe an action in progress in the past that was interrupted by another action), and the simple past (to describe a completed past action).

■ Books open. Explain the task, and tell students this is a true story of a possible sighting of a *yeti*, a mysterious creature said to live in the Himalayan mountains.

■ Have students work alone or in pairs to write the correct form of the verb in parentheses. Circulate to give hints (e.g., "Which action occurred first? Was that action completed?"). Answer any vocabulary questions.

■ Check answers by calling on students to read a few sentences at a time out loud.

Answers

In December of 1950, mountain-climbing guide Sen Tensing **was coming** down a mountain path in Nepal when he and his friends **saw** a hairy creature in the snow. The men **hid** behind a rock. When Sen Tensing **came out**, after the creature **had disappeared** back down the trail, he found giant footprints the creature **had left** in the snow. Nearly a year later, Sen Tensing and two English mountain climbers **found** more large tracks while they **were exploring** the

(procedure continues on next page)

area around Mt. Everest. The men believed these tracks **had been made / were made** by a *yeti*, which some people think is a relative of Bigfoot. Or is there another explanation?

B *Pair work* Books open. Explain the task. Then put students into pairs to tell stories and ask questions. Circulate to provide help as needed.

■ Have each pair join another pair to take turns telling their stories and asking questions. You may want to call on volunteers to tell their stories to the class.

Optional activity

Group work **Role play** Books closed. Put pairs together to create role plays about a sighting or an encounter with a mysterious creature. Students can either write out a script or brainstorm ideas for a situation to act out impromptu. Encourage them to incorporate the vocabulary from Exercise 2 and the emotions from Exercise 6 into their stories. Give groups some time to practice, and then have them perform their role plays in front of the class or another group. (10 minutes)

5 Travel World

Topic/function: Cross-cultural experiences; describing customs

Grammar: Expectations – *(not) expected to, (not) supposed to, (not) customary to, (not) acceptable to*

Summary

Chris Brooks hosts this documentary sequence about culture shock by introducing us to different customs around the world. First, reporter Fátima Nolan speaks with two people in Brazil and asks about the countries they visited and what they experienced. Camilla talks about visiting Sweden, where she tried to greet people in the Brazilian way, by kissing on both cheeks. The Swedes were very surprised. In Sweden, people shake hands as a greeting. Mônica talks about visiting Japan and experiencing an earthquake. She noticed that the Japanese people didn't seem to panic because earthquakes occur there frequently. She says that if an earthquake were to occur in Brazil, people would panic because they happen infrequently there. Next, we travel to Peru, where reporter Denise Arregui interviews two people. Sally, from the Philippines, explains that in her culture, it is not acceptable for couples to display affection in public. She feels uncomfortable and embarrassed when she sees couples kissing in public in Peru. Andrew, from the United States, describes the differences in the bus systems: In the U.S., bus systems are run by municipalities, and fares are set, but in Peru, there are many private bus companies which compete with each other for passengers. Finally, we visit Mexico, where reporter Hilary García talks with two people. Monie, from the U.S., says she has noticed that Mexican teachers dress more professionally at school. She says that in the United States, teachers dress more casually. Finally, Delfino, from Mexico, who is married to an American, describes his surprise at lunch one day when his wife prepared him a small meal – typical in the United States. However, in Mexico it is customary to eat a very large meal in the middle of the day. Chris Brooks says good-bye by hoping that the viewers have something to think about the next time they travel abroad.

Preview

1 CULTURE

Practically every person who spends an extended period of time in another country or culture experiences some degree of culture shock. The culture preview in the Video Activity Book prepares students to learn about different cultures by introducing the concept and the three stages of culture shock.

■ Books closed. Ask, "What is culture shock? What does a person who experiences culture shock feel?" Accept all answers.

■ Books open. Have students read the information in the culture preview silently. Answer any vocabulary questions.

■ Ask, "How many stages of culture shock are there? What happens in each stage?" Let students volunteer the information.

■ Put students into groups of three or four to discuss the questions. If possible, try to make sure that each group contains someone who has visited another country or region of his or her own country. Call on selected students to share some of their group's answers.

Optional activity

***Group work* Further discussion questions**
Books open or closed. Write the following statement and questions on the board or read them aloud to the class:

Some people think that any kind of major transition (e.g., starting college, getting married, moving house, beginning a new job) involves the same three stages that occur during culture shock.

(procedure continues on next page)

1) *Do you think this is true? Why or why not?*
2) *Make a list of some major life transitions.*
   Discuss any that you or someone you know
   has experienced.

Put students into groups of four or five to discuss
the questions. When the discussions are over,
call on volunteers to share their experiences.
(15 minutes)

2 VOCABULARY *Travel abroad*

These activities ask students to categorize words
associated with foreign travel and encourage
them to think of additional words to categorize.

■ Books open. Explain the task, and lead
students through the words and the categories in
the word map.

■ Have students work alone to sort the words
into the proper categories, and then have them
compare answers with a partner.

■ Check answers around the class by asking,
"What vocabulary words are associated with
customs?", etc., and having students volunteer
answers.

Answers
Customs
eating a huge meal at lunch
kissing in public
shaking hands

Feelings
confused
embarrassed
uncomfortable

Scenery
beautiful
picturesque
spectacular

Optional activities

A *Pair work* **Additional words** Books open.
Explain the task, and have students work in
pairs to add more words to each category. Then
put two students together to share answers. Call
on one member from each group to share their
additional words with the class, and write the
new words on the board. (10 minutes)

Possible answers: additional words
Customs
bowing
driving on the left side of the road
exchanging business cards

Feelings
uncertain
nervous
relaxed

Scenery
mountainous
wooded
remarkable

B *Group work* **Using words in context**
Books open. Write the following sentences on the
board:

1) Custom: *I think _____ might be a custom
   in _____ (country).*
2) Feeling: *I feel _____ when _____ .*
3) Scenery: *_____ (place) looks _____
   to me.*

■ Have students work in pairs to write one
sentence like the ones above for each vocabulary
word in Exercise 2. Circulate to help as needed.

■ Put pairs together, and have students take
turns reading their sentences aloud, but without
the vocabulary word. The other pair tries to
guess what word they were thinking of.
(15 minutes)

3 GUESS THE FACTS

In this activity, students make predictions about
the causes of culture shock described in the
sequence.

■ Books open. Explain the task, and lead
students through the words. Then have students
check their guesses and compare guesses with a
partner.

■ Call on selected students to share their
predictions with the class. At this point, do not
tell students which answer is correct, but explain
that they will find out the answers in Exercise 4.
(The answers are given in Exercise 4 of this
book.)

Optional activity

***Class activity* Further predictions** Books closed. Play the sequence with the sound off for one and a half minutes (until just before reporter Fátima Nolan speaks). Ask, "What country do you think *Travel World* visits first?" Have students volunteer their guesses; tell them that the answer will become clear during the next activity. (The first country *Travel World* visits is Brazil.) Then play the sequence with the sound off for another minute (until the interview with Camilla is over). Then ask, "What type of custom from Exercise 3 do you think this young woman is talking about?" If the class cannot guess, tell them the answer (greetings). Ask, "What two different kinds of greetings do you think she is describing?" (kissing on both cheeks; shaking hands). If the class cannot guess, tell them they will discover the answer as they continue to work with the sequence in the next exercise. (5 minutes)

 **Watch the video**

4 *GET THE PICTURE*

In the first activity, students watch and listen to check the predictions they made in the preceding exercise. In the second activity, they watch and listen to gather information about the people interviewed in the sequence.

A Books open. Explain the task, and make sure students understand that they should look back at Exercise 3 to check their predictions as they watch the sequence.

■ Play the entire sequence with the sound on. Have students work alone as they watch to check and, if necessary, correct their predictions from the previous exercise.

■ Circulate to check answers, and replay the sequence if necessary before giving the answers.

Answers
clothing, food, transportation, dating customs, and greetings

B Books open. Explain the task, and lead students through the pictures and names.

■ Play the entire sequence with the sound on, and have students fill in the information about each person.

■ Find out if anyone needs to watch the sequence again, and replay as needed.

■ Ask students to compare answers with a partner, and then check answers around the class.

Answers
Camilla
Lives in Brazil; visited Sweden

Mônica
Is from Brazil; visited Japan

Sally
Is from the Philippines; lives in Peru

Andrew
Is from the United States; lives in Peru

Monie
Is from the United States; lives in Mexico

Delfino
Is from Mexico; lives in the United States

5 *WATCH FOR DETAILS*

In this activity, students focus more closely on details in order to match the name of the country to its custom.

■ Books open. Explain the task, and lead students through the list of countries and statements.

■ Have students predict the answers before viewing the sequence and then compare predictions with a partner.

■ Play the entire sequence with the sound on, and have students check their predictions.

■ Ask if anyone needs to view the sequence again, and replay as necessary. Then have students compare answers with a partner.

■ Check answers around the class.

Answers
1) Sweden
2) Peru
3) Mexico
4) the United States
5) the Philippines
6) Brazil

6 *WHAT'S YOUR OPINION?*

In these activities, students personalize the information presented by ranking how uncomfortable a custom or situation in a new country would make them feel, and then talking about their reactions to the customs with a partner.

A Books open. Explain the task, and read the phrases aloud with the class.

▪ Have students rank the customs and situations.

B *Pair work* Books open. Explain the task, and read the example language. Then put students into pairs to take turns talking about the customs and situations.

▪ Call on selected pairs to share their conversations with the class.

Optional activity

Pair work **Cross-cultural role play** Books open or closed. Write the following prompts on the board:

1) a Swedish person visits Brazil
2) a Mexican student attends a university in the U.S.
3) a Peruvian couple visits the Philippines

Put students into pairs, and ask each pair to think about one of the above scenarios, or a similar one of their own choosing. Have them discuss what kinds of cross-cultural differences the travelers might notice and what problems they might encounter. In each pair, Student A plays the part of a reporter and Student B plays the part of a traveler who has just returned from a trip. The reporter asks the traveler about what cultural differences he or she noticed and whether he or she experienced any difficulties. After pairs have practiced their role plays, have them present their scenarios to the class or another pair. (15 minutes)

Follow-up

7 *CROSSING CULTURES*

In this communicative activity, students extend the topic by talking about different customs in a country they know about.

A Books open. Explain the task, and go over the chart. Students complete the chart individually. Circulate to help with vocabulary as needed.

B *Pair work* Books open. Explain the task. Put students into pairs, and give them a few minutes to talk about the customs in the countries they chose. Then call on selected students to share their partners' customs with the class.

Optional activity

Group work **Not following the customs**
Books open. Write these questions on the board:

1) Which customs do you think would be most difficult for a foreign traveler to guess?
2) Which customs do you think would be most difficult for a foreign traveler to adapt to?
3) For each custom, explain what you think the locals' reaction would be if someone didn't follow that custom.

▪ Put two of the pairs who worked together in Exercise 7 together. Have each pair read the three questions about the customs in their charts to the other pair. (15 minutes)

Language close-up

8 *WHAT DID HE SAY?*

This cloze activity has students focus on specific language used by Chris Brooks to explain the concept of culture shock.

▪ Books open. Have students work alone to fill in as many blanks as they can before watching the sequence. Then have students compare predictions in pairs.

■ Play this segment of the sequence through once, and have students work alone to check their predictions and fill in the blanks as they watch.

■ Have students compare answers with a partner. Then ask if anyone needs to watch the video again, and replay as necessary.

■ Play the segment once more as a final check so that students can check their answers.

■ Check answers around the class by asking students to take turns reading sentences, or by reading the answers yourself.

Answers

Hi, I'm Chris Brooks. **Welcome** to *Travel World*. Have you ever **traveled** to a **country** with a **completely** different **culture**? If you have, you **probably** know what "**culture shock**" is. It's a feeling of **confusion** you get from **suddenly** being in a new **environment**. The **traditions** and **customs** may seem **strange**. **Expectations** are different. You don't know exactly what you're **supposed to** do. You may **even** be a little **bit afraid** of making a **mistake**. In **time**, you get **used to** everything. But **when** you get **home**, you often have some **interesting** and perhaps **humorous** stories to **tell** about your **cross-cultural** experiences.

Optional activity

***Pair work* Defining culture shock** Books closed. Put students into pairs. Have students take turns telling their partners what culture shock means in their own words. Tell students to include one or two examples from the video or their own knowledge to illustrate the points. (5 minutes)

---

9 *EXPECTATIONS* Describing customs

In these activities, students practice the grammatical focus of the unit by using phrases that express expectations to describe customs in Sweden and Japan.

■ Books open. Explain the task, and read through Camilla's and Mônica's notes and the phrases to express expectations with the class.

■ Have students work alone to write sentences expressing advice to prospective visitors. Then have students compare answers with a partner. Remind students that there are several possibilities for each answer.

■ Check answers around the class by having selected students read aloud one sentence at a time. Accept any answers that are grammatically correct and make sense.

Possible answers

1) In Sweden, you're expected to be punctual.
2) In Sweden, you're not supposed to drink until the host or hostess has made a toast.
3) In Sweden, it's not customary to have emotional arguments.
4) In Sweden, you're expected to bring a cake to work on your birthday.
5) In Japan, you're supposed to take off your shoes before entering someone's home.
6) In Japan, it's not acceptable to use soap in the bathtub.
7) In Japan, it's customary to bow when you meet someone.
8) In Japan, you're not supposed to eat in public.

Optional activity

***Group work* Worldwide customs quiz** Books open. Put students into groups of three. Have each group write as many sentences like those in Exercise 9 as they can in ten minutes, about countries all over the world. Then put each group with another. Have students take turns reading their sentences, but without mentioning the country. The other group members try to guess which country has that custom. (15 minutes)

6 Heartbreak Hotel

Topic/function: Hotel complaints; describing problems; making complaints

Grammar: *Need* with passive infinitives and gerunds

Summary

Walt, the manager of a hotel, needs to run some errands. He asks Eddie, the janitor, to keep an eye on things while he is out. Mike and Kim arrive to stay for the weekend, and they check in with Eddie. He then changes clothes to act as the bellboy and shows them around their room. After he leaves, Mike and Kim find several problems with the room: the window won't shut and the heater is broken. They call the front desk to complain, and Eddie (now dressed as a maintenance worker) comes to make repairs. After he leaves, Mike and Kim find that the window is stuck shut, the heat is stuck on high, and there is no running water. The phone doesn't work, so they can't call the front desk. They decide to leave the hotel and ask to see the manager. To their surprise, it's Eddie again. They ask for their money back and leave the hotel. After they leave, Walt comes back and asks Eddie if anything happened while he was gone. Eddie assures him that he was able to take care of everything.

 **Preview**

1 CULTURE

Bed and breakfasts, or B & Bs, are popular with weekend travelers and vacationers who wish to enjoy some charm and personal attention during a stay away from home. B & Bs are often historic homes that have been remodeled, and it is not unusual for the owners to join their guests for breakfast, which is included in the price of the room. The culture preview in the Video Activity Book shows a quaint home that has been remodeled into a bed and breakfast. This is probably the kind of place Mike and Kim, in the video sequence, wish they had gone to.

■ Books open. Have students cover the text and look at the picture. Ask the class, "What is this?"

■ If students can't guess that it's a hotel, tell them. Then ask, "How is this different from a traditional hotel? Why might someone choose to stay here instead of in a traditional hotel?" Have students raise their hands to share their answers with the class.

■ Have students read the information in the culture preview silently. Then have students underline the reasons people choose to stay in a bed and breakfast.

■ Have students read the questions following the culture information. Put students into groups to discuss their answers to the questions. If you have students of different nationalities in your class, ask someone from each group to tell about some of the different types of hotels in other countries they learned about.

Optional activity

Group work **Hotel facilities and services**
Books closed. Have students, working in groups of three or four, make a list of facilities and services commonly found in hotels (conference rooms, swimming pool, room service, gift shop, etc.). Circulate to provide help with vocabulary. Write these categories on the board: *Business travelers, Families, Single travelers.* Call on one member from each group to add their group's facilities and services to the appropriate category on the board. (10 minutes)

2 VOCABULARY *Problems*

In this activity, students practice using adjectives formed from participles to complete sentences that describe problems. Then they match the problems with a picture.

■ Books open. Explain the task, and read the words in the box and the example sentence.

■ Have students work alone to complete the sentences. Then have them compare answers with a partner.

■ Check answers around the class by calling on students to read completed sentences aloud.

Answers

1) dirty	5) cracked
2) peeling	6) stuck
3) stained	7) wrinkled
4) scratched	8) freezing

■ Give students time to look at the pictures. Then have students work individually to match a sentence to a picture.

■ Direct students' attention to your book, and point to each picture. Ask students to call out the sentence that describes the picture.

Answers (from left to right)

6	4	2	1
8	3	5	7

Optional activity

Pair work **Word extension** Books open or closed. Put students into pairs to take turns asking, "What else can be (dirty)?" Circulate to answer questions and provide ideas, if necessary. (5 minutes)

Possible answers

dirty
kitchen
dormitory
garage

peeling
wallpaper
label

stained
any article of clothing
carpet

scratched
wooden furniture
a painted metal surface

cracked
window
plate
bowl

stuck
door
drawer

wrinkled
articles of clothing
sheets

freezing
an unheated room
a car in winter

---

3 GUESS THE STORY

In this activity, students prepare to work with the video by using visual information to predict what happens in the sequence.

■ Books open. Explain the task, and lead students through the photos and choices.

■ Have students work individually to answer the three questions. Then ask them to compare answers with a partner.

■ Check predictions around the class, and accept all answers. Tell students that they will find out the answers when they watch the video.

Answers
1) The manager is leaving.
2) The couple is here to relax.
3) The couple doesn't like the room.

 **Watch the video**

4 GET THE PICTURE

In this activity, students watch and listen to the entire sequence to identify problems with Mike and Kim's hotel room.

■ Books open. Explain the task, and lead students through the information in the chart. Then play the entire video with the sound on, and have students check off their answers as they watch.

■ Have students compare answers with a partner. Then ask if anyone needs to watch again in order to complete the task, and replay as needed.

(procedure continues on next page)

- Check answers around the class.

Answers
1) broken
2) peeling
3) scratched
4) stuck
5) dirty

Optional activity

Pair work **Finding more problems** Books open or closed. Tell students there are three additional problems with Mike and Kim's room mentioned in the sequence. Put students into pairs, and play the sequence again so they can find the additional problems. Call on pairs to identify the three additional problems.
(5 minutes)

Answers
The window is stuck.
The curtains are torn.
There is no running water.

---

5 WATCH FOR DETAILS

In this activity, students focus more closely on details to identify descriptions of Mike, Walt, Kim, and Eddie.

- Books open. Explain the task, and have students fill in as many of the sentences as they can before watching the sequence again.

- Play the entire sequence again with the sound on. Have students work alone to complete the sentences. Then have students compare answers with a partner. Play the sequence again if necessary.

- Check answers by calling on students to read the sentences aloud. If any students made mistakes, play the sequence again, and pause the video at the problem point.

Answers
1) Walt   5) Mike
2) Kim   6) Eddie
3) Mike   7) Kim
4) Eddie   8) Walt

6 WHAT'S YOUR OPINION?

In this activity, students discuss the theme of the unit – problems with hotel facilities and service – and give their opinions about the situation in the sequence and similar situations in their own lives.

- ***Pair work*** Books open. Explain the task, and read the questions to the students. Then put students into pairs to discuss the questions. Tell pairs to assign one person to take notes during their discussion.

- Have each pair join another pair to take turns sharing their answers to the questions. Tell the partners who took notes to help fill in details of the discussion.

Optional activities

A ***Group work*** **More questions** Books closed. Write these questions on the board:

1) *Do you think it's a good idea to find a hotel on the Internet?*
2) *Can you tell when you walk into a hotel if the service will be good?*
3) *Would you rather stay in a quaint little hotel or a big fancy hotel? Why?*
4) *What kinds of problems can guests cause hotel employees?*

Give students a few moments to think about their answers. Then put students into groups of three or four to discuss the questions. Circulate to provide help as needed. Then lead a group discussion. (10 minutes)

B ***Pair work*** **Solutions** Books closed. Put students into pairs, and ask them to think of solutions that either Eddie or Walt could have offered Mike and Kim (e.g., a different room, a discount on a future stay, or a complimentary night's stay). Circulate to provide help. Call on pairs to read their solutions to the class, and write them on the board. Have the class vote on the most popular solution, the most creative, etc. (5 minutes)

7 ROLE PLAY Describe the problems

In these activities, students extend the language of describing problems to a restaurant scene, and then role-play the problems and solutions.

A *Pair work* Books open. Explain the task, and give students time to look at the picture.

■ Put students into pairs to list the problems they see. Circulate to help out with vocabulary.

■ Call on selected pairs to identify the problems they found, and list them on the board.

Possible answers
The plate is cracked.
The tablecloth is dirty and torn.
The food is burned.
The wine glass is broken.
The waiter's jacket is dirty.
The ceiling is leaking.
The window glass is cracked.
The table has bugs crawling on it.
The chandelier is broken.
The soup has a fly in it.
The menu has stains on it.
The children are noisy.
The restaurant has mice.

B *Group work* Books open. Explain the task, and read the example language. Then have each pair join another pair to form a group of four. Tell groups to assign roles and begin the activity. Tell students to role-play as many of the problems as they can from the list on the board from part A, making sure everyone has a chance to play the role of the waiter.

■ Circulate to provide help and check on accuracy. Then call on selected groups to present one of their role plays to the class.

Optional activity

Group work **More role plays** Books closed. Put students into new groups of three or four to create a problem/solution scenario for one of the following:

passengers on board a ship and a ship's steward
passengers on an airplane and a flight attendant
passengers waiting at an airport and an airline
   employee
customers at a store and a store clerk

Have students brainstorm problems and solutions together, and then assign roles for the role play. Give each group sufficient time to rehearse, and then have groups perform their role plays for another group or the whole class. (10 minutes)

8 WHAT DID THEY SAY?

This cloze activity develops bottom-up listening skills by focusing students' attention on specific language used by Mike and Kim to complain to Eddie toward the end of the sequence.

■ Books open. Have students, working individually or in pairs, fill in as many blanks as they can before watching the video.

■ Play this segment of the sequence as many times as necessary. Have students work alone to check their predictions and fill in the blanks as they watch.

■ Have students compare answers with a partner. Then replay this segment of the sequence so that students can check their answers against the video.

■ Ask if anyone needs to watch part of the segment again to check their answers. Replay requested segments as necessary.

■ Check answers around the class, and then play the segment again as a final check.

(procedure continues on next page)

- Model the conversation or, if you wish, lead a choral or individual repetition of it to prepare students to work in groups of three. Then put students into groups of three to practice the conversation.

Answers

Mike: We are **leaving**!

Eddie: Is there something the **matter**?

Mike: **Everything**'s the matter! First of all, the **temperature** control is still **broken**.

Kim: The room was **freezing**. Now it's **too hot**, and we can't **control** the heat.

Mike: The window is **stuck** – again. Now we can't **open** it.

Kim: There's no **water**, and even the **telephone** doesn't work.

Mike: In fact, **nothing** works! Everything is in need of **repair**. I want to see the **manager**.

Eddie: Of course, sir. Just a **minute**.

Mike: Can you **believe** this place? What **else** can go wrong?

Eddie: What **exactly** is the **problem**, folks?

---

9 NEED *WITH PASSIVE INFINITIVES AND GERUNDS*
Describing problems

In these activities, students use cues from Eddie's list of things to do to describe problems using passive infinitives and gerunds. Then they personalize the activity by talking about problems in their own environments.

A Books open. Explain the task, read Eddie's list aloud to the class, and explain any vocabulary if needed.

- Have students work alone to write sentences about what needs to be done. Remind students to write two sentences for each item on the list.

- Have students compare answers with a partner. Then check answers with the class.

Answers

1) The heat needs adjusting / needs to be adjusted.
2) The wastebasket needs emptying / needs to be emptied.
5) The rooms need cleaning / need to be cleaned.
4) The hair dryer needs fixing / needs to be fixed.
   or
   The hair dryer needs repairing / needs to be repaired.
3) The chair needs repairing / needs to be repaired.
   or
   The chair needs fixing / needs to be fixed.
6) The floors need washing / need to be washed.

B Books open. Explain the task. Be sure to tell students that it is OK to make up chores that need to be done if they are having difficulty thinking of things. Circulate to help with vocabulary as needed.

- Put students into pairs to share their sentences. Then call on selected students to take turns writing their sentences on the board.

Optional activity

Pair work **Other problems** Books open. Put students into pairs. Have them make sentences with *need + passive infinitive or gerund* about the picture in Exercise 7. Circulate to help with additional vocabulary as needed. Have pairs join another pair to take turns reading their sentences. Then call on volunteers to write their sentences on the board. (10 minutes)

7 Saving Florida's manatees

Topic/function: Conservation; describing environmental problems and solutions

Grammar: The passive and prepositions of cause

Summary

As the sequence opens, we see a group of tourists in Florida taking a boat trip across a lake. Suddenly, they see an animal in the water – a manatee. The narrator gives some general information about manatees and explains that the United States government and the state of Florida have declared the manatee an endangered species. Manatees have been killed or injured by watercraft, and their habitat has been reduced by development. Park rangers from the Crystal River National Wildlife Refuge and Homosassa Springs Wildlife Park, where manatees are protected, talk about the habits of manatees and the threats they face. A park ranger also reports about the migratory habits of manatees and how researchers at the Florida Marine Research Institute are studying their migratory patterns. Scientists at SeaWorld® discuss efforts to rescue injured manatees, rehabilitate them, and return them to the wild. The narrator closes by noting that the manatee population has been increasing recently, which is a sign that their environment is being better cared for. The Web address, www.savethemanatee.org, is provided for viewers who would like to find out more about manatees and how to save them.

 *Preview*

1 CULTURE

As the population in the United States grows and development spreads, people must take an active role in helping animals whose lives and/or habitats are being endangered by human activities. The culture preview in the Video Activity Book builds student interest in the topic by presenting information about how state and national parks in North America can help preserve wildlife.

■ Books closed. Ask, "How can state and national parks protect wildlife?" Accept all answers.

■ Books open. Have students read through the culture preview silently and, as they read, circle things parks are doing to preserve North America's wildlife.

■ Ask selected students what they circled, and encourage them to explain which preservation measures they think are the most helpful. Then go over the information in the culture preview, and answer any questions about vocabulary or content.

■ Read the questions with the class, and put students into pairs or small groups to discuss them.

■ Call on selected students to share some of their group's answers. If time permits, have students change pairs or groups and discuss the same questions.

(see next page for an optional activity)

Optional activity

Group work Further discussion questions
Books closed. Write these two questions on the board:

1) *What animals are endangered in your country?*
2) *What are some things that governments can do to help endangered animals?*

▪ Put students into groups, and tell them to write one or two more questions about endangered species to add to your questions. When groups finish their questions, have each group write their questions on the board.

▪ Tell groups to choose two or three of the questions to discuss. Circulate to help with vocabulary.

▪ Ask several groups to share their discussions with the class. (15 minutes)

2 VOCABULARY *Environment*

In this activity, students practice vocabulary for talking about the environment by matching words with pictures.

▪ *Pair work* Books open. Explain the task, and lead students through the words in the box, the pictures, and the example. You may want to model the words and have students repeat. Put students into pairs to match the words with one of the pictures.

▪ Have pairs compare answers with others. Go over the answers with the class.

Answers
1) refuge
2) conservation
3) pollution
4) natural environment
5) predator
6) development

Optional activity

Pair work **Classifying vocabulary words**
Books open. Ask the class, "Which of the items in Exercise 2 could harm an endangered species? Which items could help an endangered species?" Put students into pairs to discuss their choices. Encourage them to give reasons for their answers. Ask pairs to think of one or two additional factors that could harm or help an endangered species.

Possible answers
Could harm an endangered species: pollution, predator, development
Could help an endangered species: refuge, conservation, natural environment
Call on pairs to share their additional factors, and write them on the board. (10 minutes)

3 GUESS THE FACTS

In this activity, students prepare to watch the video by making predictions about different factors that pose a threat to manatees.

▪ Books open. Explain the task, and explain vocabulary if necessary. Have students work alone to check their guesses.

▪ Have students compare predictions with a partner. Encourage them to give reasons for their guesses.

▪ Call on selected students to share their predictions with the class. At this point, do not tell students which answers are correct, but explain that the answers will become clear as they continue to work with the sequence. (The answers are given in Exercise 4 of this book.)

Optional activity

Class activity **Further prediction** Books closed. Play the video with the sound off for 30 seconds (until the scenes of manatees swimming under water). Then ask, "Do you think manatees are dangerous to people?" Ask students to write down their prediction, and tell them that they will discover the answer after watching the entire sequence. (Manatees are not dangerous to people.) (5 minutes)

 *Watch the video*

4 GET THE PICTURE

In this activity, students watch and listen to check and, if necessary, revise the predictions they made in the previous exercise. Then they identify the activities carried out by different organizations to save the manatee.

A Books open. Explain the task, and have students look back at the predictions they made in Exercise 3.

▪ Play the entire sequence with the sound on, and have students check and correct their predictions while viewing.

▪ Have students compare answers with a partner. Then check answers around the class, and replay the sequence if necessary.

Answers
Manatees are threatened by boats, development, fishing lines, and pollution.

B Books open. Explain the task, and have students look at the four pictures.

▪ Play the entire sequence with the sound on, and have students match what each organization does with its picture.

▪ Have students compare answers with a partner. Then ask if anyone needs to watch the sequence again, and replay as necessary.

▪ Go over the answers with the class.

Answers
Crystal River National Wildlife Refuge
3) They provide a natural warm-water habitat for manatees in the winter.
Homosassa Springs Wildlife Park
4) They teach visitors how manatees are being threatened.
Florida Marine Research Institute
1) They study places wild manatees swim to in summer months.
SeaWorld®
2) They rescue and help injured manatees.

Optional activity

Pair work **Who works where?** Books closed. Write these names on the board: *Betsy Dearth, Dr. Buddy Powell, Eileen Nuñez, Randy Runnells*. Play the sequence again, and ask students to note where each person works. Have students compare answers with a partner, and replay the sequence if necessary. Then check answers around the class. (10 minutes)

Answers
Betsy Dearth: Homosassa Springs Wildlife Park
Dr. Buddy Powell: Florida Marine Research Institute
Eileen Nuñez: Crystal River National Wildlife Refuge
Randy Runnells: SeaWorld®

5 WATCH FOR DETAILS

In this activity, students focus more closely on details in order to complete sentences about manatees.

▪ Books open. Explain the task, and lead students through the list of statements. Explain that the missing words are all numbers. Give students a few moments to write down guesses of what the numbers are. Call on selected students to share their guesses, and write some of the guesses on the board.

▪ Play the entire sequence with the sound on, and have students work alone to fill in the blanks.

▪ Ask if anyone needs to view the sequence again, and replay as necessary. Then have students compare answers with a partner.

▪ Check answers around the class. Ask if anyone came close to guessing the right answers.

Answers
1) 60
2) 1,000; 10
3) 60
4) 2,600
5) 46
6) 2; 4
7) 30

(procedure continues on next page)

Optional activity

Class activity **Manatee trivia quiz** Books closed. Write the following numbered words and phrases on the board in a column:

1) the elephant
2) a smooth circle on the water
3) Amanda
4) Belize
5) as many as 20 a year
6) the Save the Manatee Club

Tell students that these are *answers* to a quiz about manatees, and they must write questions which match the answers. If you wish, let students try to write questions before watching the sequence again and compare questions with a partner. Play the entire sequence with the sound on, pausing as necessary for students to write their questions. Replay the sequence as necessary. Call on selected students to write their questions on the board. Encourage students with different questions to call out their questions as you write them. (15 minutes)

Possible answers
1) What is the closest living relative of the manatee?
2) What do you see when a manatee swims near the surface of the water?
3) What is the name of a manatee at Homosassa Springs Wildlife Park who got hit by a boat?
4) In what other country does Dr. Buddy Powell study manatees?
5) How many manatees does SeaWorld® rehabilitate each year?
6) What organization can give you more information about how you can help manatees?

6 GUESSING MEANING FROM CONTEXT

In this activity, students use context clues to figure out the meanings of words used in the sequence.

■ Books open. Explain the task, and read the statements with the class. Model the exercise by showing students how to use clues in other parts of the sentence to figure out the meanings of the underlined words (e.g., In the first sentence, the

word *pollution* lets students know that *made dirty* is the correct answer.).

■ Have students work alone to make their guesses. Then put students into pairs to compare their answers. Encourage them to point out to their partners which words in the sentences they used as clues.

■ Check answers around the class.

Answers
1) made dirty
2) low body temperature
3) nose
4) plans
5) restore

Optional activity

Group work **Vocabulary tic-tac-toe** Books open. Put students into groups of three. One student is the caller. Tell the caller to write down any nine vocabulary words from Exercises 2 and 6 on a slip of paper and number them (1–9). Be sure the caller does not show the other two group members the words. Then tell the caller to draw a tic-tac-toe grid on a piece of paper and number each square (1–9). To play, the other two group members take turns calling out a number. The caller reads the corresponding word from the slip of paper, and the player must define the word and use it in a sentence. If the player is correct, he or she writes his or her initials in the square. If the player is incorrect, the square remains in play. The first player to initial three squares in a row wins. If neither player claims three squares in row, then the winner is the player who captures the most squares. If time permits, let each student have a turn as caller. (10 minutes)

 *Follow-up*

7 A CONSERVATION PLAN

In this communicative activity, students discuss conservation plans to help save an endangered animal.

A ***Pair work*** Books open. Have students look at the pictures of the animals and brainstorm reasons why they are endangered or threatened.

Below is some background information on the endangered or threatened animals pictured in Exercise 7. Use this information to help students brainstorm plans for conservation. (*Note:* This information does not appear in the Video Activity Book.)

snow leopard
The snow leopard from Mongolia is listed as endangered. Farms are encroaching on the snow leopard's habitat. In search of food, leopards prey on domestic livestock. Farmers kill the leopards to protect their livestock.

bald eagle
Once endangered, the bald eagle of North America is currently listed as threatened. Its threatened status is due to the loss of important habitat to development.

giant panda
The giant panda from China is an endangered species. Its endangered status is due to the loss of important habitat to development and quickly growing human populations.

rhinoceros
The rhinoceros is an endangered species from both Africa and Asia. Hunters kill them for their horns. Some cultures believe that the powdered rhino horn will cure everything from fever to food poisoning.

gorilla
The gorilla is an endangered species from Africa. The gorilla's habitat is being destroyed by deforestation due to logging. Gorillas are also threatened by human-transmitted diseases and by hunters who kill them to sell as valuable "bush meat."

■ Explain the task, and put students into pairs to choose an animal and list their plans. Tell students they may choose an animal from the pictures or one of their own. Circulate to help with vocabulary if necessary.

B *Group work* Explain the task, and read the example language. Put pairs together to share their ideas.

■ Call on selected students from each group to present their group's suggestions to the class.

Optional activities

A *Pair or group work* **Creating a wildlife park** Books closed. Put students into pairs or small groups. Tell them they will plan a wildlife park for an area they are all familiar with, such as the place they are living now. Students should describe the park, decide what kinds of animals they will include in the park (they do not need to be endangered), and what kinds of programs and services their park will feature. Then put groups together to share their ideas, or have groups explain their ideas to the whole class. (15 minutes)

B *Group work* **Debate** Books closed. Write one or both of these debate topics on the board:

1) *The government should set aside large areas of land solely for animals.*
2) *Zoos are a good place for endangered animals to live.*

■ Put students into groups of four, and ask them to choose a topic. Then divide the groups into two pairs. One pair will think of arguments that support the topic, and the other pair will think of arguments against the topic.

■ When they have finished gathering ideas, put the two pairs together to discuss the topic. Have groups work independently, or have them debate their topic in front of the class. (15 minutes)

Language close-up

8 *WHAT DID THEY SAY?*

This cloze activity has students focus on specific language used in the sequence to explain the importance of saving the manatees.

■ Books open. Have students work alone to fill in as many blanks as they can before watching the sequence. Then have students compare predictions in pairs. Play this segment of the sequence through once, and have students work alone to check their predictions and fill in the blanks as they watch.

(procedure continues on next page)

- Have students compare answers with a partner. Then ask if anyone needs to watch the video again, and replay as necessary.

- Play the segment once more so that students can check their answers.

- Check answers around the class by asking students to take turns reading sentences, or by reading the answers yourself.

Answers

Narrator: So why is it **important** to continue to spend so much **time** and **money** on this seemingly insignificant creature? **Perhaps** it has to do with our own well-being.

Man: I think they're kind of like a **sign** of how the **environment**'s doing. And if manatees can **survive** alongside us, I think our environment's going to be doing **well**.

Woman 1: We're not only providing and **protecting** habitat for a **wildlife** species, but we're also **preserving** a healthy habitat for **ourselves**.

Woman 2: **We're** the ones that **have to** do something about it; otherwise, our **children** and their children might not see **manatees**.

9 PASSIVE; PREPOSITIONS OF CAUSE *Describing environmental problems and solutions*

This activity has students work with both the topic and the grammatical focus of the unit by using the passive and prepositions of cause to make sentences about environmental problems and solutions.

- Books open. Explain the task, and read through the sentences. Model the first sentence by asking students to call out the correct passive sentence as you write it on the board. Then point out the two options for categorizing the sentences.

- Have students work alone to rewrite the sentences and classify them as problems or solutions. Have students compare answers with a partner.

- Check answers around the class by having selected students read aloud one sentence at a time. Have them say whether the sentence is about an environmental problem or solution.

Answers

1) Injured and endangered animals are being helped as a result of the work of volunteers all over the world.
2) The quality of life for some manatees is being improved through stricter pollution controls.
3) The habitat of many wild animals has been reduced because of development.
4) A large number of manatees have been injured by fast-moving watercraft.
5) The air has been contaminated due to exhaust from cars and smoke from factories.

8 Salsa!

Topic/function: Salsa dancing; talking about learning methods

Grammar: Gerunds and infinitives

Summary

In this documentary sequence, reporter Billy Kimmel speaks to salsa dancers to find out why salsa is popular, how they learned the dance, how they improved their dancing, and what advice they have for others who would like to learn. First, he visits a dance studio in Tokyo. He interviews some salsa students who tell him why they began taking salsa lessons and how they improved their skills – by going out to nightclubs and practicing hard. He next travels to a dance studio in Seoul, Korea, where some salsa dancers advise those wanting to improve their dancing to practice with a good partner, or just to move to the music. Finally, he visits the Quest Dance Club in the United States. There, he speaks to a teacher and some regular visitors to the club. The teacher recommends taking group or private lessons and then practicing. Some of the club visitors talk about the wide appeal of salsa – it has a driving beat and a lot of passion, and it's a fun type of partner dance without a lot of steps to learn. It's also a mix of different trends and cultures, which appeals to many people. They also talk about good ways to learn salsa: It's important to take the initiative – take a class, or just watch and listen to the music, and then try it. Of course, it's important to practice. Finally, Billy takes a few lessons and closes the sequence by demonstrating some salsa steps himself.

 **Preview**

1 CULTURE

Learning to dance is a popular activity all over the world. The sequence focuses on salsa dancing. Salsa is a blend of different types of music and is fashionable in many countries all over the world today. The culture preview in the Video Activity Book builds interest in the topic by giving some background information about salsa music and having students think about why people like to dance.

■ Books closed. Ask, "What kind of music began around the 1930s in New York City and is a blend of music from the Caribbean islands, Latin America, and Africa?"

■ If students can answer "Salsa music" and know something about salsa music, ask them to share their knowledge with the class before reading the culture preview to learn more. If students are unable to answer, say, "Well, let's learn about this kind of music."

■ Books open. Have students read the information in the culture preview silently and underline one new thing that they learn about salsa music. When they finish, ask, "What did you learn?" and have a few volunteers answer. Then answer any content or vocabulary questions.

■ Put students into groups of three or four to discuss the questions as you circulate.

■ Bring the class back together, and have selected students share their discussions with the class.

2 VOCABULARY Learning

In these activities, students practice vocabulary for talking about learning by matching verb phrases to their corresponding words or phrases, and then by using the new phrases to complete sentences.

A *Pair work* Books open. Explain the task, and go over the lists with the class.

▪ Put students into pairs to match the verbs with the appropriate words or phrases. Then have each pair compare their answers with another pair.

▪ Check answers around the class by calling on one student to read the first part of each phrase and another to complete it. Give the class time to make any necessary corrections.

Answers
1) decide to take lessons
2) earn a diploma
3) brush up on my skills
4) learn how to ski
5) practice hitting the ball
6) take classes

B Books open. Explain the task, and have students work alone to complete the sentences with phrases from part A. Have students compare answers with a partner.

▪ Check answers around the class by calling on selected students to read a sentence aloud.

Answers
1) decide to take lessons
2) practice hitting the ball
3) brush up on my skills
4) take classes
5) earned a diploma
6) learn how to ski

Optional activity

Group work **Discussion questions about learning** Write these questions on the board:

1) *How many years did you spend or have you spent in school?*
2) *What was your favorite subject?*
3) *What kinds of things have you learned outside of school? How did you learn them?*

4) *Do you prefer to learn alone, with a friend, or in a class?*
5) *Talk about some ways of learning that worked well for you.*

Put students into groups of four or five to discuss the questions. Circulate to help with vocabulary as needed. When groups are done, call on each group to share one or two pieces of information they learned about each group member.
(15 minutes)

3 GUESS THE FACTS

In this activity, students make predictions about the reasons for salsa dancing's popularity and how people learn or improve salsa dancing.

▪ Books open. Explain the task, and read the two questions. Then have students work alone to make their predictions.

▪ Put students into pairs, and have students discuss their predictions with a partner.

▪ Call on selected students to share their predictions with the class. At this point, do not tell students which answers are correct, but explain that the answers will become clear as they do Exercises 4 and 5. (The answers are given in Exercises 4 and 5 of this book.)

Optional activity

Class activity **Identifying things people study** Play the video with the sound off for thirty seconds (until you see reporter Billy Kimmel). Tell students to jot down or remember as many different subjects as they can that they see people studying. Play the video again if necessary, and go over the answers with the class. (5 minutes)

Possible answers
English
computers/programming
dancing
math
chess

 **Watch the video**

4 GET THE PICTURE

In this activity, students watch and listen to identify the reasons that people give for salsa dancing's popularity.

■ Books open. Explain the task, and lead students through the statements. See if any of the statements match students' predictions from Exercise 3.

■ Play the entire sequence with the sound on for students to do the task. Have students compare answers with a partner.

■ Find out if anyone needs to watch the sequence again, and replay as needed.

■ Check answers around the class.

Answers
It's easy to do.
The music is enjoyable.
It's a mix of many trends and cultures.
You don't have to learn many steps.

Optional activity

Group work **Ranking the reasons** Have students look at the answers to Exercise 4. Ask them to rank the reasons from 1 to 4, with 1 being the most appealing aspect to them of learning salsa. Put students into groups of three or four to compare and explain their rankings. (5 minutes)

5 WATCH FOR DETAILS

In this activity, students focus more closely on details in order to identify the ways that different people in the sequence recommend learning or improving salsa dancing.

■ Books open. Explain the task, and lead students through the list of statements.

■ Play the entire sequence with the sound on, and have students match the people to their recommendations as they listen.

■ Ask if anyone needs to view the sequence again, and replay as necessary. Then have students compare answers with a partner.

■ Check answers around the class by pointing to the pictures in turn and asking, "How does he or she recommend learning or improving salsa dancing?" Call on selected students to read the matching recommendation.

Answers
1) By practicing hard.
2) By coming to class every weekend.
3) By practicing with a partner.
4) By moving to the music.
5) By going out to nightclubs and getting together with friends at parties.
6) By taking the initiative.

Optional activity

Group work **What would work best for you?** Have students look at the suggestions in Exercise 5 for learning or improving salsa dancing. Ask, "Which way do you think would work best for you? Can you think of any different ways to learn or improve salsa dancing?" Put students into groups of four or five to share their answers and ideas. (10 minutes)

6 WHAT'S YOUR OPINION?

In these activities, students personalize the information in the sequence by talking about the personal qualities that are important for learning how to dance and learning how to do other activities.

A Books open. Explain the task, and lead the class through the chart. Answer any vocabulary questions.

■ Have students work alone to rank the qualities from 1 to 9.

B *Pair work* Books open. Explain the task, and put students into pairs to take turns sharing their rankings from part A and to discuss the different activities.

■ To extend the exercise, make new pairs, or put pairs together, and repeat the exercise.

Follow-up

7 ADVICE TO LEARNERS

In these communicative activities, students extend the topic of the unit by listing ways that people could learn an activity, and then asking and answering questions about that activity in a group.

A Books open. Explain the task, and have students choose an activity and list ways to learn it in the chart. Circulate to help out with vocabulary as needed.

B *Group work* Books open. Put students into groups of three or four. Explain the task, and read the example language. Then have students take turns talking about their activities, while group members ask questions. Encourage students to ask follow-up questions.

Optional activity

Pair work **Interview role play** Have students work with a partner who was not in their group for part B. One student role-plays a reporter who interviews the other student about how he or she learned an activity. Let students practice their role play several times, and then have students present their role play to the class. If time permits, have students switch roles.
(15 minutes)

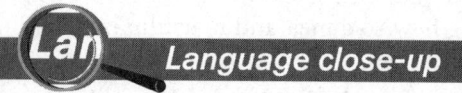

Language close-up

8 WHAT DID THEY SAY?

This cloze activity has students focus on specific language used by a salsa dancer to explain to host Billy Kimmel why she thinks salsa is popular and how she likes to learn it.

■ Books open. Have students work alone to fill in as many blanks as they can before watching the sequence. Then have students compare predictions in pairs.

■ Play this segment of the sequence through once, and have students work alone to check their predictions and fill in the blanks as they watch.

■ Have students compare answers with a partner. Then ask if anyone needs to watch the video again, and replay as necessary.

■ Play the segment once more so that students can check their answers.

■ Check answers around the class by asking students to take turns reading sentences, or by reading the answers yourself.

■ Put students into pairs to practice the conversation.

Answers

Billy: You seem to be **enjoying** yourself. Do you come here **often**?

Woman 5: Yes. I come here just about **every** week. I come here to **dance**.

Billy: Why do you **think** salsa is so **popular**?

Woman 5: You don't **learn** a set of **steps**. You just **listen** to the music and **interpret** the music.

Billy: What's the best **way** to learn salsa **dancing**? Any **recommendations**?

Woman 5: **It depends** on how you **learn**. Some **people** learn best by going to a **class**. I learn best by **watching** and listening to the music and then getting **brave** and **trying** it a little.

Billy: Do you **prefer** taking lessons in a **studio** or **going** out to a club?

Woman 5: I prefer **coming** to a club and dancing here. There's a different **energy**; it's more **social**. But there's nothing **wrong** with taking lessons. I **recommend** it.

Optional activity

Pair work **Interview** Put students into pairs to role-play Billy Kimmel interviewing someone about the popularity of salsa and how to learn to dance salsa. "Billy Kimmel" should read the lines as written in Exercise 8, and the "salsa dancer" should change the responses, either by using information given in the sequence or by using his or her own ideas. Let pairs practice their interviews several times and then present them to the class. (10 minutes)

9 GERUNDS AND INFINITIVES
Talking about preferences

In these activities, students practice both the functional and the grammatical focus of the unit by using gerund or infinitive phrases to talk about preferences.

A Books open. Explain the task, and lead students through the first question.

■ Have students work alone to write the questions, and then put students into pairs to compare questions with a partner.

■ Check answers around the class by calling on selected students to read aloud one question at a time.

Answers
1) Would you prefer to earn a diploma or learn for fun?
2) Would you rather learn English in Australia or in Canada?
3) Would you prefer to learn how to cook or learn how to dance salsa?
4) Would you rather brush up on skills you already have or learn something new?
5) Would you rather read English magazines or English novels?
6) Would you prefer to study in the morning or at night?

B *Group work* Books open. Explain the task, and have students work in groups of four or five to ask and answer the questions from part A.

■ Call on students to share one or two pieces of information they learned about their classmates.

Optional activity

Class activity **Class survey** Books closed. Have each student write a question about preferences, following the patterns in Exercise 9. Then have the class stand and circulate. Have each student read their question to every other student and note the response. When everyone has finished, give students a few minutes to tally the answers, and then call on selected students to summarize the responses for the class (e.g., "Twelve people in our class would rather take a vacation at the beach. Eight people would rather go to the mountains."). (15 minutes)

9 Stress relief

Topic/function: Stress; making suggestions

Grammar: Gerunds, infinitives, base-form verbs, and negative questions

Summary

This sequence opens with Margie, an office worker, complaining to her co-worker John about how stressed she feels. He sympathizes and offers her a number of different solutions, such as exercise, yoga, and aromatherapy. For every solution, though, Margie has an objection; she either doesn't like the activity, can't do it, or has had a bad experience with it. She does admit that hypnotherapy helped her – in fact, it was too effective, and now whenever she hears the word *ocean*, she drifts off to sleep. After his other recommendations are turned down, John ends by suggesting to Margie that she take a trip – to the ocean. At the sound of the word *ocean*, Margie begins to get sleepy.

 **Preview**

1 CULTURE

Stress is the reaction of our bodies and minds to something that upsets their normal balance. A good example of stress in action is the way you react when you are frightened or threatened. Your body's defense mechanisms release adrenaline – your heart pounds, your blood pressure rises, your muscles tense, and the pupils of your eyes open wide. This "fight or flight" response readies your body to either resist (fight) or retreat (take flight).

In North America, workers frequently mention stress as one of the most difficult aspects of their jobs. Workers suffer from both physical and mental stress that can lead to illness, injury, or "burnout." Stressed people may look for physical solutions, such as physical therapy, massage, and exercise, or mental solutions, such as relaxation techniques, meditation, and counseling. The sequence shows John and Margie discussing various ways of dealing with stress that have been popular in the past ten years. The culture preview in the Video Activity Book prepares students to work with the unit by introducing the topic and presenting information about stress and its effects.

■ Books closed. To introduce the topic, ask the class, "What is stress? What kinds of things cause stress?" Ask for volunteers to call out answers as you write them on the board.

■ Books open. Have students read the culture preview silently to check their predictions. Then answer any questions about vocabulary or content.

■ Put students into groups of four to answer the discussion questions.

■ Bring the class back together, and have selected groups report their answers to the class.

Optional activity

Group work **Stress reduction** Books closed. Put students into groups of three to design a relaxation or stress reduction activity for the whole class (e.g., a simple exercise, or a guided relaxation). Have each group or a representative from each group lead the whole class through their "relaxation." (10 minutes)

2 VOCABULARY Stress

In this activity, students practice using different idiomatic expressions related to stress that are used in the sequence.

■ Books open. Explain the task, and lead students through the expression box and paragraph. Answer any questions students may have.

- Have students work alone or in pairs to complete the paragraph. Encourage them to first fill in the expressions they are sure about, and then to go back and guess at the ones they are not sure about.

- Check answers by calling on students to read sentences aloud, or read the paragraph aloud yourself.

Answers

Last year, I felt so **stressed out** by my job. Every day it seemed like I was **under pressure** from my boss. I used to **blow off steam** by complaining to my co-workers, but that didn't work – it only made them feel stressed, too! One day, someone in my office brought me a brochure from a health club. "This complaining **has got to stop**," she said. "Why don't you **take some time off** from work and **take up** exercising?" It turned out to be just **the right thing for me**. My co-workers were so happy about how relaxed I was when I came back. They told me never to forget how important it is to take care of myself. **You can say that again!**

- If time permits, put students into pairs to take turns reading the paragraph aloud to each other. Circulate to help with pronunciation and intonation.

Optional activity

Pair work **Further practice** Books open. Put students into pairs to write new sentences for each of the expressions. For "You can say that again!", point out that they will need to write a complete sentence beforehand, since that expression is a response to someone else's statement. Have each pair join another pair to take turns reading their new sentences aloud, saying "blank" in place of the vocabulary expression. The other pair guesses the expression that completes the sentence. (15 minutes)

---

3 GUESS THE STORY

In this activity, students use visual information to predict answers to two general questions about the people in the sequence.

- Books open. Explain the task, have students look at the photo of Margie in her office, and read the two questions.

- Have students work alone to write their predictions, and then have them compare predictions with a partner.

- Check predictions around the class. Accept all answers, but encourage students to explain how they made their predictions. Be sure not to confirm answers at this point. Instead, tell students they will find out the woman's problem and what the man is telling her when they watch the entire sequence. (The woman feels stressed; the man is giving her suggestions about how to relax.)

Optional activity

Class activity **Further predictions using visual cues** Books closed. Play the entire sequence with the sound off. Ask if any students wish to change their earlier predictions. Then ask, "What activities are the two people discussing? Why do you think they are talking about those activities? What do you think happens at the end of the sequence?" Accept all answers, but do not give any correct answers at this point. (10 minutes)

 **Watch the video**

4 GET THE PICTURE

In this activity, students watch and listen to the entire sequence to identify and then discuss the activities that John suggests to Margie.

A Books open. Explain the task, and give students time to look at the illustrations. You may wish to read the words below the illustrations and have students repeat. Explain any unfamiliar vocabulary, if necessary.

- Play the entire sequence with the sound on. Have students check their answers as they watch and then compare answers with a partner.

- Ask if anyone needs to watch the sequence again, and replay as needed.

(procedure continues on next page)

■ Check answers by asking, "Does John suggest (aromatherapy)?" and call on selected students or volunteers to answer, "Yes, he does" or, "No, he doesn't."

Answers (from left to right)
aromatherapy, taking a trip
dance lessons
hypnotherapy, swimming, yoga

B *Pair work* Explain the task, and put students into pairs. Have students take turns talking about the activities they have tried and the activities they would like to try.

■ Call on pairs to share their discussions with the class. If time permits, write two columns on the board: *Have tried, Would like to try*. For each activity illustrated, take a tally. Which activity has been tried by the most students? Which activity would students most like to try?

Optional activities

A *Group work* **Talking about activities**
Books open or closed. Put students into groups of four. Ask students who have tried any of the activities to share their experiences with their group. Encourage group members to ask follow-up questions. If students have difficulty thinking of follow-up questions to ask, write some examples on the board, such as:

Was it difficult?
Was it relaxing?
Would you do it again?
Would you recommend it to me?
(10 minutes)

B *Class activity* **Class survey** Books open or closed. Have each student choose one method for relaxation from Exercise 4 or one of their own. Then have the class stand up and circulate. Encourage students to speak to as many classmates as they can to get their opinions of the activity by asking questions such as, "Have you ever tried (yoga)? If so, did you like it? Why or why not? If not, would you like to try it? Why or why not?" Tell students to take notes on the information they receive. After they finish, give students time to organize their information, and then have them present summaries to the class.

Write useful expressions on the board, such as:

Most people in this class have tried swimming.
  About half of them like it.
Two people said they don't plan to try it, because
  they don't know how to swim.

Be sure to write the example language on the board. (15 minutes)

5 *WATCH FOR DETAILS*

In this activity, students watch and listen more closely to determine why Margie didn't like John's solutions to stress.

■ Books open. Explain the task to students, and give them time to read all of the sentences.

■ Play the entire sequence with the sound on. Have students work alone to answer the questions as they watch.

■ Replay the sequence if necessary, and then have students compare answers with a partner.

■ Check answers by calling on pairs of students to ask and answer, "Why doesn't Margie like (Rollerblading®)?" "Because she got hurt." If students make any mistakes, replay the sequence and pause at the problem area.

Answers
1) She got hurt.
2) She couldn't find a good partner.
3) She can't swim.
4) It's probably not the right thing for her.
5) It worked too well.
6) Perfume makes her sneeze.

Optional activity

Class activity **Listening for idioms** Books closed. Have students turn to Exercise 2. Play the sequence again, and tell students to raise their hands each time they hear one of the idioms listed in the box about stress. Replay the sequence as many times as necessary.
(10 minutes)

6 *WHAT'S YOUR OPINION?*

In the first activity, students give reasons why Margie might reject some additional activities. In the second activity, students perform a role play of John giving Margie additional suggestions for coping with her stress, and Margie turning them down.

A *Pair work* Books open. Explain the task, and lead students through the activities. Explain any vocabulary, if necessary. Then put students into pairs.

■ Give students time to write the reasons Margie might give for rejecting the activities. Circulate to help with vocabulary. Then have each pair join another pair to compare reasons.

B *Pair work* Explain the task, and read the example language. Have students take turns role-playing John and Margie. Encourage them to use appropriate tones of voice (e.g., John sounding sympathetic and Margie sounding stressed and unenthusiastic).

■ To extend the practice, have students change partners and repeat the exercise.

Optional activity

Pair work **Personalization** Books open. Put students into new pairs. Have them take turns suggesting the activities from part A, but have Student B give his or her own answers. (5 minutes)

Follow-up

7 *HOW STRESSED ARE YOU?*

In the first activity, students personalize the topic by discussing with a partner how much stress they feel in certain situations. In the second activity, they survey the class about the same situations.

A *Pair work* Books open. Explain the task, and lead students through the chart. Point out the example language, and model it with a student.

■ Give students time to add one more idea to the chart and to check (✔) their answers in the chart. Circulate to answer any questions.

■ Put students into pairs to take turns asking and answering the questions. Encourage students to add at least one more sentence that gives further information or an explanation to their answer.

B *Class activity* Explain the task. Then have students stand and circulate, writing down classmates' answers. You may wish to take part in the activity yourself.

■ Ask the class, "What things are the most stressful for our class? What things are the least stressful for our class?"

Language close-up

8 *WHAT DID THEY SAY?*

This cloze activity develops listening skills by focusing students' attention on specific language used by Margie and John in the beginning portion of the sequence.

■ Books open. Explain the task. Then have students, working individually or in pairs, read the conversation and fill in as many blanks as they can before watching the sequence.

■ Play this segment of the video as many times as necessary while students work alone to check their predictions and complete the task. Then have students compare answers with a partner.

■ Check answers around the class. Then play the segment again as students follow along in their books and check their work.

■ Model the conversation or, if you wish, lead a choral or individual repetition of it. Then put students into pairs to practice the conversation.

Answers
Margie: Ah! This has **got to** stop.
John: What is it, Margie? You look so **stressed out**.
Margie: John, it's this **job**. I'm under **pressure** all the time. My muscles are **tense**. My stomach is **upset**. I just can't seem to **relax**. What can I do?

(answers continue on next page)

John: Yeah, **stress**. It's a **killer**. Well, one **thing** you could do is exercise. It really **helps** me when I'm **stressed out**, and it's a great way to **blow off** steam.

Margie: Well, **actually**, I've tried that. **First** I took up Rollerblading®, . . . but that **didn't work**. Then I tried **dancing** lessons, . . . but I couldn't find a good dance **partner**.

9 SUGGESTIONS

In this activity, students practice the grammatical and functional focus of the sequence by creating, making, and responding to suggestions.

A Books open. Explain the task, and lead students through the expressions and sentences. Answer any questions.

▪ Have students work individually to write a suggestion for each of John's problems. Encourage students to use different expressions for each suggestion. Circulate to provide help as necessary.

▪ Call on volunteers to share their answers with the class.

Possible answers
1) Have you thought about listening to Spanish CDs while you're doing something else?
2) It might be a good idea not to answer your phone.
3) Why don't you reschedule your vacation?
4) What about going to a museum?
5) One thing you could do is to start reading earlier.

B *Pair work* Explain the task. Then give students a few moments to write their two problems.

▪ Put students into pairs to take turns reading their problems and offering suggestions. Call on each pair to present one conversation to the class, or put two pairs together to share their problems and suggestions.

Optional activity

Class activity **Suggestion box** Books closed. Write these seven problems, each on a separate slip of paper:

1) I can't finish my homework on time.
2) I can't get to sleep at night.
3) I don't know where to go on vacation.
4) My best friend tells my secrets.
5) I lost my wallet.
6) I can't remember people's names.
7) I want to be a fluent English speaker.

Then tell students to prepare seven blank slips of paper to write their solutions down. Read a problem aloud, and have each student write a suggestion on a slip of paper and give it to you. Read all the suggestions aloud, and have the class vote for the best, the most creative, and the funniest suggestion. (15 minutes)

10 Fort Steele Heritage Town

Topic/function: Living historic villages; talking about the past

Grammar: Referring to time in the past with adverbs and prepositions

Summary

This documentary sequence shows how the living historic village of Fort Steele Heritage Town recaptures the spirit of an 1890s Canadian frontier town. As scenes from the old Fort Steele are shown, the narrator explains how Fort Steele was founded and settled, and how it became deserted in 1898. In 1961, interested community members started Fort Steele Heritage Town to preserve the site and offer exhibits and demonstrations of frontier life to the public. We meet some of the employees from Fort Steele Heritage Town who play the parts of such people as a Royal Canadian Mounted Police Officer (a Mountie), a blacksmith, a schoolteacher, and a short-distance hauler. We see the insides of traditional shops and stores. At the close of the sequence, General Manager Martin Ross predicts that as Canadians become more interested in their history, Fort Steele Heritage Town will become more popular and will expand by adding additional attractions.

 **Preview**

1 CULTURE

Living historic villages in North America resemble towns from long ago, with many original or restored streets and buildings. Costumed actors play the parts of people from the village and act as guides for visitors, demonstrating traditional crafts and explaining what life was like long ago. The culture preview in the Video Activity Book builds student interest in the topic by giving information about living historic villages such as Fort Steele Heritage Town.

■ Books closed. Tell the class that this unit is about a living historic village, and ask, "What do you think that is?" If students do not know the answer, tell them it is a village that shows visitors what life was like in the past. Then ask, "What are some ways you think this is done?" Accept all answers.

■ Books open. Have students read the culture preview silently and underline ways in which living historic villages show a certain time in history. Answer any vocabulary questions.

■ Ask several students to tell the class what they underlined and why. Then lead students through the questions, and put them into pairs or groups to answer the questions as you circulate.

■ Have various students share their answers with the class.

2 VOCABULARY Life long ago

In this activity, students work with vocabulary for describing life in the 1890s by matching items with illustrations.

■ Books open. Explain the task, and have students look at the six illustrations. Lead students through the words in the box. Then have students work alone to match the words to the correct illustrations.

■ Have students compare answers with a partner. Then check answers around the class by holding up the book and asking, "What is this picture?"

Answers (from left to right)

frontier town	ferry	miner
pump	blacksmith	wagon

(see next page for an optional activity)

Optional activity

Pair work **Vocabulary classification** Books open. Write these categories on the board: *People, Places, Equipment.* Put students into pairs, and tell them to put each word from Exercise 2 into one of the three categories. Then, put pairs together to share their answers. Check answers around the class by calling on selected pairs. (5 minutes)

Answers

People	*Places*	*Equipment*
blacksmith	frontier town	ferry
miner		pump
		wagon

3 GUESS THE FACTS

In this activity, students prepare to watch the sequence by making predictions about why settlers in North America moved west in the late 1800s.

■ Books open. Explain the task, and then have students work alone to write their predictions. Tell students that they may write several predictions.

■ Call on selected students to share their predictions with the class. At this point, do not tell students which answer is correct, but explain that they will check their answers when they watch the sequence. (The settlers moved west to seek their fortunes in the gold fields and to claim land for farms and ranches.)

Optional activity

Class activity **Vocabulary reinforcement** Books open. Play the video with the sound off for two minutes (until General Manager Martin Ross speaks). Have students work alone to make a list of any vocabulary words from Exercise 2 that they see represented. Call on selected students to share their answers, and then play the segment again. As the sequence plays, have students call out what they see. (5 minutes)

Answers
wagons, Mounties, blacksmith, frontier town, ferry, miners

 *Watch the video*

4 GET THE PICTURE

In these activities, students watch and listen to the entire sequence to describe the duties of different jobs at Fort Steele by matching job titles and descriptions to illustrations.

A Books open. Explain the task, and have students look at the photos.

■ If you wish, have students work in pairs to predict the answers before watching the sequence.

■ Play the sequence with the sound on. Tell students to match each job with a picture by writing a number in the box. Then have students compare answers with a partner.

■ Ask if anyone needs to watch the sequence again, and replay if necessary before going over the answers with the class.

Answers (from left to right)
3 2 1 5 4

B Books open. Explain the task, and have students work alone to predict the answers before watching the video.

■ Play the sequence with the sound on. Have students work alone to check their predictions as they watch and then compare answers with a partner.

■ Check answers around the class. Then have students practice asking and answering in pairs (e.g., "Who taught grades one through eight together in two rooms?" "The schoolteacher."). The student answering should try to answer with the book closed. Have students switch roles, and ask and answer the questions again.

Answers
1) schoolteacher
2) Mountie
3) blacksmith
4) general manager
5) short-distance hauler

5 *WATCH FOR DETAILS*

In this activity, students focus more closely on details in the sequence to decide whether statements are true or false and to correct false statements.

■ Books open. Explain the task, and go over the example. Then lead students through the list of statements. Answer any questions about vocabulary or content.

■ Have students predict whether each statement is true or false and then compare predictions with a partner before viewing.

■ Play the entire sequence with the sound on. Have students work alone to check their predictions and mark each statement as true or false as they watch and listen.

■ Ask if anyone needs to view the sequence again, and replay as necessary. Then have students compare answers with a partner.

■ Check answers by calling on selected students.

Answers
1) False (It is located in western Canada.)
2) True
3) True
4) False (The town was deserted for more than fifty years.)
5) False (Fort Steele Heritage Town was started by interested community members.)
6) True
7) True
8) True
9) False (New attractions that might be added are a boot maker or a hatmaker.)

Optional activity

Pair work **More true/false** Books open or closed. Put students into pairs to write three statements, two true statements and one false, about the sequence. Have pairs exchange statements and then watch the sequence again to mark each statement as true or false. Then have students correct the false statements. (15 minutes)

6 *MAKING INFERENCES*

In this activity, students use the information they learned from the video to make inferences about what life was like in the 1890s.

Pair work Books open. Explain the task, and read the statements with the class.

■ Put students into pairs. Tell each pair to think of one additional question, and have pairs write their questions on the board.

■ Have students discuss the questions. Tell them to choose two additional questions to discuss from the board. Circulate to provide help as needed.

■ Call on selected pairs to share their answers.

Possible answers
1) People washed clothes by hand.
2) They grew fruit and vegetables, raised farm animals, and hunted wild animals.
3) People used horses and wagons for transportation.
4) They used animals for transportation, work, and food.
5) Their houses were made of wood.

Optional activity

Group work **Discussion questions** Books closed. Put students into groups of three or four. Write the following questions on the board for groups to discuss:

1) *What would you like about living in Fort Steele in the 1890s?*
2) *What would be challenging for you?*
3) *What aspects of life then would be similar to life today?*
4) *What aspects would be the most different?*
5) *What do you think people from the 1890s would be the most surprised about in today's world?*

Have one person in each group take notes about the group's ideas to share with the class.
(15 minutes)

7 CREATE A LIVING HISTORIC VILLAGE

In this communicative activity, students work with the theme, vocabulary, and grammar of the unit by choosing a period in history and creating an imaginary living historic village to show what life was like then.

A *Pair work* Books open. Explain the task, and have students look at the pictures.

■ Put students into pairs to discuss and plan their villages. Circulate to help with vocabulary. Reassure students that they do not need to include historically accurate information; rather they should plan what aspects of the village and everyday life they would feature.

B *Group work* Books open. Explain the task, and read the example questions. Then put pairs together to ask and answer questions about their villages.

■ Call on selected students from each pair to present their pair's ideas to the class.

Optional activity

Pair work and group work **A living historic village for the future** Books closed. Put students into pairs. Explain that the year is now 2100, and they have made a living historic village about the early 2000s. On a sheet of paper, have pairs draw a simple plan of their village and mark the different sections (e.g., apartment buildings, train station, shopping mall, park). Then put pairs together, and have each pair give the other a "tour" of their village: "Here are the apartment buildings where people lived. Look at how tall they are!" The visiting pair should ask questions about the "past" such as, "What did people use for transportation 100 years ago? How did they cook their food?" Remind students to use the past tense for their questions and explanations. (15 minutes)

8 WHAT DID HE SAY?

This cloze activity has students focus on specific language used to explain the history of Fort Steele.

■ Books open. Have students work alone to fill in as many blanks as they can before watching the sequence. Then have students compare predictions in pairs.

■ Play this segment of the sequence through once, and have students work alone to check their predictions and fill in the missing words as they watch.

■ Ask if anyone needs to watch the video again, and replay as necessary.

■ Have students compare answers with a partner. Then play the segment again for a final check.

■ Check answers around the class by asking students to take turns reading sentences, or by reading the answers yourself.

Answers
Narrator: So, what was it **like** in **Canada** during the nineteenth **century**? The late 1800s were a **period** of westward expansion and **development** in Canada. Some people were **moving** west, seeking their fortunes in the **gold** fields. **Others** came to claim **land** for farms and **ranches**. The shopkeepers and tradesmen came soon after, offering **goods** and **services** to the new **settlers**. New **frontier** towns were born. Fort Steele was a **typical** town of that **period**. It began as a **ferry** crossing over the Kootenay River, providing a way for **miners** to reach the gold fields. Then, in **1898**, the Canadian Pacific Railway **located** their new rail line through the **neighboring** town of Cranbrook. **Within** a few years, the **population** of Fort Steele was **reduced** to a couple of hundred. **For** more than fifty years, the **town** was deserted.

Optional activity

Pair work **Interview** Books closed. Write these questions on the board:

1) What was Canada like during the nineteenth century?
2) How did Fort Steele begin?
3) What happened to Fort Steele?

Put students into pairs to role-play an interview between a reporter, who asks the questions, and a historian, who answers them. Give students a few minutes to mark in their books where the answers begin and end, and then have students practice the interview. If you wish, have pairs present their interviews to the class. (10 minutes)

Answers

1) What was Canada like during the nineteenth century? The late 1880s was a period . . . Fort Steele was a typical town of that period.
2) How did Fort Steele begin? It began as a ferry crossing over the Kootenay River, providing a way for miners to reach the gold fields.
3) What happened to Fort Steele? In 1989, the Canadian Pacific Railway . . .

9 *TALKING ABOUT THE PAST*

In these activities, students practice the grammatical focus of the unit by choosing words to complete a passage about Prince Edward Island.

A Books closed. Ask the class, "Does anyone know where Prince Edward Island is? What famous novel was set there?" If students don't know the answers, tell them they will find out as they complete Exercise 9.

■ Books open. Explain the task, and have students work individually to complete the paragraph. Circulate to answer questions about vocabulary and content. Then have students compare answers with a partner.

■ Check answers around the class by having selected students read aloud one sentence at a time.

■ Ask, "What did you learn about Prince Edward Island?" and call on selected students to share information.

Answers

Jacques Cartier of France was the first European to discover Prince Edward Island over 450 years **ago**. The first French settlement was built **in** 1719, and is now a national historic site. **During** the 1700s and 1880s, the island was controlled at different times by the British and the French. **From** 1769 **to** 1873, the island had an independent government; **since** then, it has been a part of Canada. Lucy Montgomery, who wrote the popular novel *Anne of Green Gables* **in** 1908, lived on the island **during** the late 1880s and early 1900s. *Anne of Green Gables* is a fictional account about life on Prince Edward Island. Tourists today can visit the home where she lived **for** thirty-five years. **After** touring the museum, many visitors stop by the bookstore to purchase copies of her novels.

B ***Group work*** Books open. Explain the task, and put students into groups of four.

■ As students are speaking, circulate and make notes of statements students use that include prepositions or adverbs to talk about the past.

■ Write some of the students' sentences on the board (do not write students' names by their sentences). When the groups have finished talking, bring the class back together and ask them to look at the sentences on the board. Ask, "Are all of the sentences grammatically correct?" If there are any mistakes, ask the class if they can correct them. If not, provide the correct answers yourself.

11 If only ...

Topic/function: Behavior and regrets; describing regrets about the past

Grammar: Time clauses with *should have* + past participle and *if* clauses + past perfect

Summary

The sequence opens on the evening of Roberta's birthday. Her friends Deanna, Amelia, Pamela, and Laura have decided to throw her a surprise party. Deanna takes Roberta out to dinner, and the rest of the young women hide in Roberta's house. When Roberta and Deanna return home, the women jump out and yell, "Surprise! Happy birthday!" The women sit down to have some cake, and Amelia opens a photo album with pictures of all the young women when they were together in college. As they look at the pictures, they talk about what they were like in college and things they wish they had done differently. Deanna thinks that she studied too much and never learned to relax, but her friends point out that her dedication helped her become a successful lawyer. Pamela regrets not having studied more but says that she is now taking business classes at night. Amelia, who hopes to be an actress, wishes she had studied education in college, so that now she could be teaching drama instead of working as a waitress. The women tease Laura for having spent so much time on the computer in college but acknowledge that this experience helped her become president of her own Internet company. Roberta announces that she has decided to become a travel agent but regrets not having studied languages in college. Then Roberta's four friends give her a birthday present – foreign language textbooks.

Preview

1 CULTURE

The culture preview in the Video Activity Book introduces and builds interest in the topic of changes and turning points in people's lives by providing some background information about changes Americans face. It also gives students the opportunity to talk about how they have changed since high school or college and to discuss turning points in their own lives.

■ Books closed. To introduce the topic, ask the class the following questions and have students respond by raising their hands:

1) Do you think people change after they leave college? In what ways?
2) What are some major changes that can occur in people's lives?

■ Books open. Have students read through the culture preview silently and underline the parts of the passage that mention the number of times the typical American moves during his or her lifetime, and the number of times the average employee changes jobs during his or her career.

■ Check the answers with the class.

Answers
The typical American moves eleven times during his or her lifetime.
The average employee changes jobs seven or eight times during his or her career.

■ Put students into pairs or groups to answer the discussion questions as you circulate.

- Bring the class back together, and have selected students each share an answer with the class. If there are students who have never moved, changed jobs, or changed a major, ask them to talk about other changes in their lives (e.g., starting school, changing grades, getting a new sibling).

Optional activity

Group work **Ten years from now** Books closed. Ask students to write down some predictions about what they will be doing in ten years. If students get stuck for ideas, suggest topics to think about, such as marital status, family, home, and job. Put students into groups of four, and have each group member write a list of predictions for each person in the group. Call on one student to go first. Have the student listen to each group member's predictions. Then have the student read his or her own predictions. Ask students to keep track of predictions that were the same. Ask for groups to share their predictions with the class and tell which predictions were the same. (15 minutes)

2 VOCABULARY *Behavior*

In these activities, students become more familiar with words that describe behavior by first matching definitions to words that describe personal characteristics, such as those of the young women in the video sequence, and then using the vocabulary to match the kind of behavior best suited for four jobs.

A Books open. Explain the task, and lead students through the words in the box and the example sentence. As you read the words in the box out loud, you may have students repeat them in chorus to practice pronunciation.

- Have students work alone to match the vocabulary words with the appropriate descriptions. Then have students compare answers with a partner.

- Check answers around the class by asking, "What do we call someone who wants to be successful?" and having students call out the answer.

Answers
1) ambitious
2) dedicated
3) sophisticated
4) realistic
5) serious
6) sensible
7) naive
8) carefree

B *Pair work* Books open. Explain the task. Then point to each of the pictures in turn, and ask, "What is this job like? What does this person do all day?" If you wish, record answers on the board as students call them out.

- Put students into pairs to choose the qualities necessary for each job. Remind students to explain their choices to their partners (e.g., "We said a Web-page designer should be sophisticated, because she will have to use new technologies and know about current trends.").

Optional activities

A *Pair work* **Additional jobs** Books closed. Have students work with a new partner. Write these new occupations on the board: *biologist, fashion designer, comedian, reporter*. Tell pairs to add two more jobs of their own to the list. Have students repeat part B with this new list of jobs. (10 minutes)

B *Group work* **Discussing personal qualities and jobs** Books open or closed. Put students into groups of three or four. Have one student use vocabulary from Exercise 2 to describe his or her behavior. The group must listen and suggest suitable jobs for that person. Tell groups to assign a secretary to record the group's suggestions and report the decisions back to the class (e.g., "We said that Ming Yee should be an architect because she's dedicated and sophisticated."). (10 minutes)

3 GUESS THE STORY

In this activity, students prepare to watch the video by using visual information to predict what the young women are doing in different situations.

- Books open. Explain the task, and give students time to look at the pictures. Have them write predictions about what the women are doing on a separate piece of paper.

(procedure continues on next page)

■ Play the video for one minute with the sound off (to where Amelia opens the photo album). Give students time to change any of their guesses, if they wish.

■ Have students compare predictions with a partner. Then check predictions around the class, and tell students that they will find out the answers when they watch the entire sequence.

Answers
1) Some women are hiding to surprise their friend.
2) The women are yelling, "Happy birthday!" to their friend.
3) The women are looking at photos of themselves from the past.

Optional activity

Class activity **Further predictions** Books closed. Have students watch the video with the sound off for one more minute (until the girls are telling Pamela she has to study). Ask students to guess what the girls were talking about (their past; their lives before), and why (they are remembering what they were like in college). Ask, "Do you like to look at photos of yourself or your friends from the past? Why or why not?" Call on selected students to share their answers with the class. (10 minutes)

 **Watch the video**

4 *GET THE PICTURE*

In this activity, students watch and listen to the entire sequence to find out general information about the five young women in the sequence.

■ Books open. Explain the task, and have students look at the photos of the five women.

■ Play the sequence with the sound on. Have students complete the chart alone as they watch and listen.

■ Tell students to compare answers with a partner, and then ask if anyone needs to watch the sequence again. Replay as needed before checking answers around the class.

Answers

Name	Now	Other (possible answers)
Deanna:	successful lawyer	was always serious
Pamela:	office clerk	is taking night classes for a degree in business administration
Amelia:	waitress	hopes to be an actress
Laura:	president of an Internet company	lost sleep in college working on computers
Roberta:	wants to be a travel agent	has traveled a lot

Optional activities

A *Group work* **More information** Books closed. Divide the class into five groups, and assign one of the young women in the sequence to each group. Have groups list as much information as they can about the woman as they watch and listen. Call on groups to report their information to the class. (10 minutes)

B *Pair work* **Alternative endings** Books closed. Have students work in pairs to imagine a different future for each young woman, based on what she was like in college (e.g., Deanna could have become a businesswoman; Deanna could have developed health problems from stress and stopped working altogether.). Encourage creativity, but remind students that they will have to defend their predictions. Have the different groups share their alternative endings and explanations with the class. (10 minutes)

5 *WATCH FOR DETAILS*

In this activity, students focus more closely on details in the sequence to complete a chart with information about the women.

■ Books open. Explain the task, and lead students through the chart. Encourage students to complete as much of the chart as they can before watching the sequence.

■ Play the entire sequence with the sound on, and have students check (✔) their answers in the chart as they watch and listen.

■ Check to see if anyone needs to view the sequence again, and replay as necessary. Then have students compare answers with a partner.

■ Check answers around the class by having students turn the statements into questions using "Who" (e.g., "Who didn't study hard in college?") and asking a neighbor.

Answers
1) Pamela
2) Laura
3) Roberta
4) Deanna
5) Roberta
6) Amelia
7) Deanna
8) Roberta

Optional activity

Pair work **Further details** Books closed. Have students work in pairs to write at least one more sentence about each woman. Play the sequence again for pairs to gather information and write their sentences. Collect the sentences, and read them aloud to the class. Have students call out the name of the woman the information describes. Save those sentences students can't answer, and write them on the board. Then replay the sequence, and ask students to call out the name of the woman that each sentence describes. (15 minutes)

---

6 *MAKING INFERENCES*

In this activity, students watch and listen more closely in order to make inferences – reach conclusions even when information is not explicitly stated – about what happens in the sequence.

■ Books open. Explain the task, and tell students that making an inference is like making a good guess based on what you know. Use the first statement as an example, if necessary. Read the statement, and then say, "Is this true or false?

How do we know?" (The women never say they were good friends in college, but they talk about their college life with obvious pleasure.)

■ Read the statements with the class, and encourage students to predict the answers before they watch the sequence.

■ Play the sequence with the sound on. Have students work alone to check their predictions and mark *True* or *False* as they watch.

■ Find out if anyone needs to view the sequence again, and replay as necessary. Then have students compare answers with a partner.

■ Check answers around the class by asking selected students to each share an answer with the class. Encourage students to give reasons or evidence from the sequence to support their answers.

■ Alternatively, check answers by playing the video with the sound on and in slow motion, if possible. Have students call out "Stop" when they hear or see evidence to support an answer. A volunteer then tells the class what the evidence is. Continue like this until you have gone over all the statements.

Answers
1) True
2) True
3) True
4) False
5) True
6) False

Optional activity

■ *Pair work* **True/false quiz** Books open or closed. Have students work in pairs to write three statements about the people in the sequence, one true and two false. Have each pair exchange statements with another pair and then watch the sequence again to mark each statement as true or false. To complete the task, have students correct the false statements and then check their answers with the pair that wrote the statements. Ask selected students to read one of their statements to the class, and have the class answer "True" or "False." (15 minutes)

Follow-up

7 CHANGES

In these communicative activities, students extend the language practice in the unit by using timelines of Amelia's life and their own lives to ask and answer questions about life events and changes.

A *Pair work* Books open. Explain the task, and lead students through Amelia's timeline by pointing to the timeline and asking, "What is this?" (a timeline); "What does it show?" (significant events in Amelia's life); "Why do you think Amelia chose those particular events?" (accept any reasonable answers).

■ Have students work in pairs to make statements about the events in Amelia's life. Before students begin, model the example language.

■ Call out one date from the timeline at a time, beginning with 1975, and call on selected students to make a statement about the date you call out.

B Books open or closed. Explain the task, and give students several minutes to create their own timelines.

■ Circulate to help students who are not sure what to include. To prompt them, ask such questions as, "Did your family ever move? When did you start a new school? When did you begin a new sport or hobby?"

C *Group work* Books open. Explain the task, and model the example language. Then put students into groups of three or four.

■ Tell students to take turns sharing their timelines. Encourage listeners to ask questions (e.g., "What happened when you moved to . . . ? How did that make you feel?"), and encourage speakers to give as much information as they can about the events they chose.

■ Ask for volunteers to present their timelines to the class.

Optional activity

Group work **Discussion questions** Books closed. Have students work in groups of three or four. Write these questions on the board for students to discuss:

1) *What were you like in high school or college?*
2) *How have you changed?*
3) *Do you still see friends from that time? How have they changed?*
4) *What is something you wish you had done differently?*

If your students are high-school age, choose a time in the past such as elementary school. Call on selected pairs to share their discussions with the class. (15 minutes)

Language close-up

8 WHAT DID THEY SAY?

This cloze activity has students focus on specific language used in conversation among the five women.

■ Books open. Have students work individually or in pairs to fill in as many blanks as they can before watching the sequence. Then have students compare predictions in pairs.

■ Play this segment of the sequence through once, and have students work alone to check their predictions and fill in the blanks as they watch.

■ Have students compare answers with a partner and then watch this segment of the video again.

■ Go over the answers with the class. Then replay the sequence as students follow along in their books and check their work.

■ Put students into groups of five to practice the conversation. If your class does not divide evenly, have one student in a smaller group read both Roberta and Pamela, or Amelia and Laura.

Answers
Roberta: Oh, look at Deanna: always the **serious** one.
    Amelia: Even then, you were **hard** at work.

Deanna: I know. I **should have been** more carefree like the rest of you. I never **learned** to relax.

Laura: Oh, but you were so **sensible**. You always did well in school and **graduated** at the top of your class.

Roberta: Yeah. Now **look** at you. You are a **successful** lawyer.

Deanna: Yes, but I didn't think that **having** a good time in college was **important**. The moment I graduated, I **realized** I **had missed** a lot. I still don't know **how to** relax and have **fun**.

Pamela: Well, Deanna, if I **had listened** to you, I **wouldn't be** just a clerk at the office. **I'd be** the manager.

9 *PAST CONDITIONALS*

In these activities, students practice both the functional and the grammatical focus of the unit by using past conditionals to discuss regrets and speculations about the past.

A Books open. Explain the task, and lead students through the example sentence. Then have students work alone to complete the exercise.

■ Have students compare answers in pairs. Circulate to provide help as needed.

■ Call on selected students to read their sentences or write them on the board.

Possible answers
1) If I had studied harder, I might have received a scholarship.
2) If you had studied a foreign language, you might have been able to study abroad.
3) If I had taken more summer classes, I would have finished my degree earlier.
4) If they had been more ambitious, they could have gotten better jobs.
5) If she had been more carefree, she might have had more friends.
6) If he had listened to his parents, he might have made better decisions.

B *Group work* Books open. Explain the task, and read the situations. Then put students into groups of three or four to discuss the situations. Encourage students to use complete sentences as they talk (e.g., "If I had been born a man, I wouldn't have worn dresses to school.").

■ Tell groups to each assign a secretary to write down the group's ideas.

■ When groups finish their discussions, have each group's secretary share a few ideas about each situation with the class.

Optional activities

A *Group work* **Additional discussion questions** Books closed. Put students into new groups of four or five, and tell them to write one additional situation to discuss on a slip of paper. Be ready with some suggestions if groups can't think of additional situations (e.g., you had chosen another job or school; you had or hadn't had a brother or sister; you had or hadn't started studying English). Circulate to provide help with accuracy. Collect the slips of paper, and hold them in your hand or put them in a hat. Have each group draw a slip of paper and discuss the situation on the slip. (10 minutes)

B *Group work* **Round robin** Books closed. Put students into groups of four or five, and if possible, have them put their chairs in a circle. Tell each student to write the first half of two *if* clauses (e.g., *If I hadn't been late . . .* , *If I had remembered to call my friend . . .* , etc.) on separate slips of paper. Be sure to tell students to leave plenty of space after their *if* clauses so that the clauses can be completed. Have students pass their slips of paper to the left. Tell students to complete the *if* clauses. When you are sure everyone has finished, have students pass their slips to the left again. Continue like this until students receive their own *if* clauses. Call on students to read their completed sentences to the class. If you hear any mistakes with verb tenses, write the incorrect sentences on the board, and ask the class to correct them together after every student has had a chance to read. (15 minutes)

12 Need information? AskJeeves.com

Topic/function: An Internet company; discussing what makes a business successful

Grammar: Infinitive clauses and phrases of purpose

Summary

In this documentary sequence, employees from the Internet company Ask Jeeves explain what makes their Internet search engine special as well as successful. Vice President of Ideas Penny Finnie and Content Editor Marjorie Stout explain that Ask Jeeves differs from other Internet search engines in that it returns a list of questions in response to a user's question in order to more accurately direct the user to sites specific to his or her needs, instead of returning just a long list of sites. Ask Jeeves was started in 1995 by a computer scientist and a venture capitalist who decided to make the Internet a more human experience by having a character on their search engine that users could interact with. The company created Jeeves the butler, a character based on the title character of a series of books written by P.G. Wodehouse beginning in the 1920s. Wodehouse continued to write novels with the Jeeves character through the 1970s. John Perry, Senior Marketing Writer, describes some of the successful marketing campaigns that have featured the character of Jeeves. Marjorie Stout and Content Editor Monte Luke stress that in addition to clever marketing campaigns, Ask Jeeves has been successful because of their efforts to ensure that the search engine returns the most useful sites for answering a user's question. Steve Roop, Director of Sales, explains the three ways in which Ask Jeeves generates revenue: by charging companies that advertise their products and services on the Ask Jeeves Web site; by charging companies who wish to be listed with the search engine; and by licensing its technology to major corporate Web sites. Ask Jeeves seems to have the answers to running a successful business – and maybe to your questions as well!

Preview

1 CULTURE

Internet use has grown rapidly in recent years. Many users rely on search engines to help them navigate the Web and find the information they are looking for. The culture preview in the Video Activity Book raises student awareness and interest in the topic by providing background information and statistics about the most popular uses of the Internet.

■ Books closed. Write the following on the board:

sending and receiving e-mail
surfing
looking for general information

Tell the class, "In a recent survey on Internet use, these were the top three reasons respondents gave for why they used the Internet. Which do you think was the most popular? the second most popular? the third most popular?" Give students time to write down their predictions. Then ask, "What other reasons for Internet use do you think the respondents gave?" Accept all answers.

■ Books open. Have students silently read the information in the culture preview and check the answers to their predictions. Answer any vocabulary questions.

■ Put students into groups of three or four to discuss the questions. If you have students who have not used the Internet or computers before, try to put them in a group with other students who have Internet experience.

■ When groups have finished discussing, call on selected students to each share some of their group's answers.

Optional activity

Group work **Further discussion questions**
Books closed. Write these discussion questions on the board:

1) *How many hours a week do you use the Internet?*
2) *Do you or any of your friends have a personal home page? What is it like?*
3) *Does your school or company have a Web site? What is it like?*

Put students into groups of three or four (if possible, different groups from the ones which discussed the questions in the Video Activity Book) to discuss the questions. Call on selected students to each share some of their group's answers. (10 minutes)

2 *VOCABULARY* The Internet

In these activities, students practice using vocabulary for talking about the Internet by first completing a cloze passage and then quizzing a partner with definitions for the words.

A Books open. Explain the task, and lead students through the passage and words in the box.

Pair work Put students into pairs to complete the passage. Before reviewing the answers with the class, have two pairs form a small group to compare answers.

■ Check answers by calling on selected students to take turns reading sentences aloud or by reading the paragraph aloud yourself.

Answers

How do people use the Internet? First, **users** must **log on**, or connect their computer to the Internet. Then, once they're **online**, they type in the **Web address** of the page on the Internet they wish to visit. A few seconds later, they will see the **Web site** appear on the screen. Some pages provide **links**, which people can click on to visit related pages. When someone doesn't know which page would be most useful, he or she can use a **search engine** to suggest different sites.

B ***Pair work*** Explain the task, and go over the example language. Then put students into pairs to ask and answer questions.

Optional activity

Group work **Vocabulary extension** Books closed. Put students into pairs, and tell them to think of more words related to Internet use. After five minutes, put pairs together to share their words. Then call on each group to share two of their new words, and write these on the board. Go over new vocabulary with the class, and give students a chance to copy it down if they wish. (10 minutes)

3 *GUESS THE FACTS*

In this activity, students predict what kind of Web site Ask Jeeves is, and what service it provides.

■ Books open. Explain the task, and have students work alone to make their predictions.

■ Have students compare predictions with a partner. Encourage them to give reasons for their guesses.

■ Call on selected students to share their predictions with the class. At this point, do not tell students which answer is correct, and if you have students who are already familiar with the Ask Jeeves Web site, ask them not to give away the answer. Explain that the answer will become clear as they continue to work with the sequence. (Ask Jeeves is an Internet search engine.)

Optional activity

Class activity **Further prediction** Books open. Play the video with the sound off for thirty seconds (until the computer cursor is put on the picture of Jeeves). Say to the class, "This Web site is called Ask Jeeves. Who do you think Jeeves is?" Accept all answers, but do not reveal the correct answer until students have watched the entire sequence with the sound on in Exercise 4. (5 minutes)

(see next page for possible answers)

Possible answers

Jeeves is the symbol of Ask Jeeves. He is a helpful butler, based on a character created by author P.G. Wodehouse in the 1920s.

 *Watch the video*

4 GET THE PICTURE

In these activities, students watch and listen to match each interesting fact about Ask Jeeves to the correct illustration and summary phrase.

A Books open. Explain the task, and lead students through the four statements.

- Have students work alone to match the statements to the illustrations before watching the sequence.

- Play the entire sequence through with the sound on. Have students check their predictions and compare answers with a partner.

- Check answers around the class by pointing to each picture and asking, "What does this picture show?" Call on selected students to read the matching statement.

Answers (from left to right)

3   1
4   2

B Books open. Explain the task, and lead students through the summary phrases.

- Have students work alone to match the phrases to the illustrations. Point out that they can use the statements from part A to help. Then have students compare answers with a partner.

- Check answers around the class by asking, "Which picture shows a clever marketing idea?", etc., and having students point to the appropriate illustration in their books.

Answers (from left to right)

a good concept   a clever marketing idea
a revenue source   a unique search engine

5 WATCH FOR DETAILS

In this activity, students watch and listen more closely in order to correct mistakes in a summary of the sequence.

- Books open. Explain the task, and read through the summary with the class. Go over the sample correction, and make sure students understand that the summary contains several other mistakes that they need to correct.

- Have students work alone to correct as many of the mistakes as they can before watching the sequence. Then have students compare answers with a partner.

- Books closed. Play the entire sequence with the sound on.

- Books open. Have students work alone to check their predictions and correct the other mistakes in the summary. Have students compare answers with a partner.

- Ask if anyone needs to see the sequence again, and replay as necessary. If students are having difficulty, let them watch the sequence with their books open.

- Check answers by reading the summary aloud as it appears in the Video Activity Book and by telling students to call out "No" and correct you when they hear a mistake.

Answers

The character of Jeeves, a helpful **butler**, has been used in several marketing campaigns. In the Butler Blast, a group of **actors** is hired to attend events like the opening of a mall. These gentlemen help people with their **shopping**, give directions, and hand out free things. Jeeves has also been a **balloon** in the Macy's Thanksgiving Day Parade. Once, the company created labels for different **fruits**. The stickers included Jeeves's face and **Web address**.

Optional activity

Pair work **Numbers quiz** Books closed. Write the following information on the board:

1) every 10–15 years
2) 1992

3) about 500
4) more than 11 million
5) 1995
6) millions and millions
7) 3

Tell students they will watch the sequence again closely to determine which questions would yield those numbers as answers. Tell them to look for visual clues as well as listen for spoken clues. As an example, give the question for the first answer yourself: "How often does the amount of knowledge in the world double?" Put students into pairs and play the sequence with the sound on for students to write their questions. More than one wording of the question may be possible. Ask if anyone needs to watch the sequence again, and replay as many times as necessary. Circulate to provide help as necessary. Call on selected pairs to read their questions to the class. (15 minutes)

Possible answers
1) How often does the amount of knowledge in the world double?
2) For what year did the user want to know the winner of World Cup soccer?
3) A few years ago, how many questions did Ask Jeeves answer in a month?
4) How many questions does Ask Jeeves answer in a month now?
5) In what year was Ask Jeeves started?
6) How many people watch the Macy's Thanksgiving Day Parade?
7) How many ways does Ask Jeeves make money?

6 WHAT'S YOUR OPINION?

In these communicative activities, students personalize the topic of the unit by asking classmates for their opinions on different aspects of Internet use.

A Books open. Explain the task, and lead the class through the chart.

■ Give students time to work alone to write their own questions for number 5.

■ Have students stand up and circulate, or have them work seated in groups of four. Have students take turns asking and answering the questions in the chart. Remind students to take notes.

B Books open. Bring the class back together. Ask students to share one or two interesting things that they learned about the other group members.

Follow-up

7 DESIGNING A WEB SITE

In these communicative extension activities, students first create their own Web site in pairs and then present it to another pair.

A *Pair work* Books open. Explain the task, point out the illustration of the Web site, and demonstrate with a quick drawing of your own "Web site" with one link, if possible.

■ Put students into pairs, and tell them to brainstorm ideas before beginning.

■ As pairs work on their Web sites, circulate to help with vocabulary if necessary. Tell students who would like to include pictures but do not feel able to draw well to simply draw squares or circles and write: *picture of x inside*. Encourage students to use different colored pens and highlighters if they have them.

B *Group work* Books closed. Explain the task, and put pairs together to take turns explaining their Web sites.

■ Pairs can either be responsible for explaining their Web sites, or they can let the other pair "discover" their Web site by asking questions such as, "What happens if I click on this link? Why did you include this picture?"

■ To extend the activity, match each pair to a new pair and let them repeat the exercise.

(procedure continues on next page)

■ As an alternative presentation, have half the pairs in the class post their Web sites on the classroom walls. The other half of the class can circulate and explore Web sites that look interesting. Post new links by holding or pinning subsequent sheets of paper over the original Web page.

Optional activity

***Group work* Marketing plans** Books closed. Put students into groups of three. Explain to the class that each group should choose one product that can be found in the classroom (including students' personal effects) and brainstorm some innovative ways to market that product (encourage them to list as many ideas as they can in five minutes). Then ask each group to decide on its two or three favorite ideas and present them to the class. The rest of the class can vote on which idea they like best. (15 minutes)

Language close-up

8 *WHAT DID THEY SAY?*

This cloze activity has students focus on specific language used by Vice President of Ideas Penny Finnie and Content Editor Marjorie Stout to explain why Ask Jeeves is a unique Internet search engine.

■ Books open. Have students work alone to fill in as many blanks as they can before watching the sequence. Then have students compare predictions in pairs.

■ Play this segment of the sequence through once, and have students work alone to check their predictions and fill in the blanks as they watch.

■ Have students compare answers with a partner. Then ask if anyone needs to watch the video again, and replay as necessary.

■ Play the segment once more as a final check so that students can check their answers.

■ Check answers around the class by asking students to take turns reading sentences, or by reading the answers yourself.

■ Put students into pairs, and have them read the parts of Penny and Marjorie. Then have them switch roles.

Answers

Penny: Most **people**, when they get on the **Internet**, don't really **know** where to go. And so they use **search engines** to find out what **sites** are out there in their areas of **interest**. Most search engines, you just go and **you type** in one **word**. So if you **wanted** to buy a car, you **would** type in *cars*. But what comes **back** is a long, long, long, long **list** of all the car sites **out there**. With Jeeves, it's **different**. Um, if you want to buy a car **online**, you go and you say, "Where can I buy a car online?" And Jeeves **takes** you to the sites that **answer** that question.

Marjorie: Ask Jeeves is **different** because it's **really** a question-and-answer **service**. You **come** to Jeeves and you ask a question. The answers we . . . we **return** to our **users** are in the form of **another** question. And so you **pick** the question that Jeeves **gives** you that's most **similar** to the one that you asked, and **behind** that question is your answer.

9 *INFINITIVE CLAUSES AND PHRASES OF PURPOSE*
Advice for a successful Web site

In this activity, students use infinitive clauses and phrases of purpose – the grammatical focus of the unit – to complete sentences about factors that make a Web site successful – the functional focus of the unit.

■ Books open. Explain the task, and lead students through the example sentence.

■ Have students work alone to complete the sentences and then compare answers with a partner.

■ Check answers around the class by having selected students read aloud one sentence at a time.

Answers
1) For/In order for
2) In order to
3) In order to
4) For/In order for
5) For/In order for

Optional activity

Pair work **E-mail advice** Books open or closed. Put students into pairs, and explain that they will use infinitive clauses and phrases of purpose to write sentences giving advice about using e-mail. Write the following example sentence on the board: *In order to get someone to open your message quickly, give it an interesting and descriptive title.* When pairs have finished or after 10 minutes have passed, bring the class back together and call on each pair to share one or two sentences. Does the rest of the class agree with the advice? (15 minutes)

13 Car trouble

Topic/function: Car trouble; offering opinions and advice

Grammar: Past modals

Summary

This sequence takes place on Sam and Emily's wedding day. Sam is being driven to the wedding by his best man, Bill. Before the sequence starts, they had just stopped at a gift shop to buy a decoration for the top of the wedding cake. Now, Sam is worried about being late; he had promised Emily he would get there early for picture taking. Bill tells him not to worry because he knows a shortcut. However, the road is under construction and they must make a detour. Meanwhile, Emily is getting worried because Sam hasn't arrived yet. Her maid of honor, Debbie, tries to reassure her. Bill drives through a field to another road but then discovers his car is having mechanical problems. Emily keeps worrying, and Debbie can't make her feel better. Bill sends Sam to a farmhouse to get some water and then sends him back to get some gas. In the end, they get a farmer to drive them to the church in his wagon. The men arrive just in time, and Bill tells Emily that Sam planned to arrive in this fashion to lend charm to an "old-fashioned" wedding.

Preview

1 CULTURE

This humorous sequence shows the problems of the groom, Sam, as he tries to get to his wedding early for picture taking before the ceremony. His bride, Emily, doesn't know what has happened to him. This sequence also features a best man, Bill, and a maid of honor, Debbie. Their roles in the wedding are to assist the groom and the bride with their wedding preparations. The culture preview in the Video Activity Book prepares students to talk about cars and the car

trouble Bill has en route to the wedding by providing interesting information about the importance of cars to the American lifestyle.

- Books closed. Ask, "What do eighty-nine percent of American households own one or more of today?" Accept all guesses. If no student guesses "cars," add, "I'll give you a hint: Their parents in the 1950s had half as many and used them half as much." See if there are any further guesses.

- Books open. Ask students to read the culture preview silently to check their predictions and find the correct answer.

- Put students into groups to answer the discussion questions. Tell groups to select one member of each group to act as secretary and write down the group's list of advantages and disadvantages, as well as any information about transportation they discussed.

- Have the secretaries report their groups' ideas to the class. Make a list on the board of the advantages and disadvantages of owning a car and the other common forms of transportation.

Optional activity

Group work **Additional discussion topics**
Books closed. Have students change groups, and write these questions on the board for them to discuss:

1) *Why do you think Americans are so fond of cars?* (possible answers: gasoline is cheaper than in many other countries; great distances between cities and towns; smaller cities sometimes have poor, or even no, public transportation; many cars are manufactured in the United States, etc.)
2) *What models of cars are popular in your country?*
3) *What kind of car would you like to own, and why?*
4) *What kinds of transportation are most appropriate for big cities? small cities? country towns? the area where you are living now?* (15 minutes)

2 VOCABULARY Car trouble

In this activity, students become familiar with vocabulary used in the sequence to describe problems with driving by matching statements with responses.

- Books closed. Ask, "What are some kinds of problems you can have when you're driving?" Accept any reasonable answers, and write students' ideas on the board.

- Books open. Explain the task, and lead students through the statements and responses.

- Have students work individually to match the statements with responses. Then have students compare answers with a partner.

- Check answers around the class.

Answers
1) d You must have gotten lost.
2) c She must have taken a shortcut.
3) e She might have had engine trouble.
4) b You might have run out of gas.
5) a He could have taken a wrong turn.

Optional activity

***Group work* Discussion questions** Books open. Take a poll to see how many students can drive, and choose one of the activities below accordingly. Tell groups to select one person in each group to act as a secretary to write down the group's ideas to share with the class later.

- **If most students can drive:** Put students into groups of four or five. Be sure that non-drivers are in a group with drivers. Tell students to take turns asking the drivers questions combining "Have you ever . . ." with the responses from column B (e.g., "Have you ever taken a wrong turn?"). If the driver answers "Yes," encourage group members to ask follow-up questions (e.g., "Where were you going? How did you find your way again?"). (10 minutes)

- **If most students cannot drive:** Put students into groups of four or five. Tell students to take turns asking questions using the responses from column B. Tell students to omit the phrase "take

a shortcut." Write this example on the board: *What could a driver do if he or she got lost?* Encourage students to think of as many possible answers as they can. When groups have finished, call on each group to share their ideas about one of the situations. (10 minutes)

3 GUESS THE STORY

In this activity, students prepare to watch the sequence by making predictions, based on visual information, about what Sam and Bill are doing, and what Emily and Debbie are thinking.

- Books open. Explain the task, and have students read the questions.

- Books closed. Play the first minute and a half of the sequence with the sound off (until Emily and Debbie finish their first conversation).

- Books open. Have students work alone to answer the questions.

- Check predictions around the class, and tell students that they will find out the answer when they watch and listen to the entire sequence.

Answers
1) They are going to a wedding.
2) The road they were driving on was closed.
3) They are worried that the men will be late.

Optional activity

***Pair work* Guessing the story** Books closed. Put students into pairs, and have each pair write at least one guess about how the story might end on separate slips of paper. Tell pairs to write their names on each slip of paper. Collect all slips of paper, and read the guesses to the class, but do not read who wrote them. After students watch the entire sequence with the sound on for Exercise 4, reveal the names of the pairs who correctly guessed the end of the story or who came closest. (Sam and Bill arrive at the wedding in a wagon – just in time.) You may want to ask the class if they liked any of the suggested endings better. (5 minutes)

 **Watch the video**

Let groups practice their role plays a few times before presenting them to the class. (15 minutes)

4 GET THE PICTURE

In this activity, students watch and listen to put the events in the proper order. Then students match sentences with the pictures they describe.

■ Books open. Explain the task. Have students cover the sentences with a strip of paper. Put students into pairs to describe to each other what is happening in each picture. Encourage students to predict as many answers as they can before watching the sequence.

■ Play the entire sequence with the sound on. Have students put the pictures in order.

■ Replay the entire sequence if necessary.

■ Put students into pairs to compare answers.

Answers (from left to right)
2   5   3
1   4

■ Have students work alone to write the correct sentence under each picture. Then have students compare answers with a partner.

■ Check answers around the class.

Answers (from left to right)
Bill drives through a cornfield.
A farmer gives Sam and Bill a ride.
Bill's car has engine trouble.

There's a "Road Closed" sign ahead.
Sam goes to get water from the farmer.

Optional activity

Group work **Reception role play** Books closed. Put students into groups of three, and tell them they will role-play a scene that takes place at the wedding reception (the party after the wedding ceremony). Give students a choice of *Role play 1* or *Role play 2*.

Role play 1: Sam and Bill explain to a guest what happened on the way to the wedding. The guest asks questions.

Role play 2: Emily and Debbie explain to a guest what they were thinking when the men were late. The guest asks questions.

5 MAKING INFERENCES

In these activities, students watch and listen more closely in order to make inferences – reach conclusions even when information is not explicitly stated – about what happens in the sequence.

A Books open. Explain the task, and remind students that making an inference is like making a good guess based on what you know.

■ Read the statements with the class, and encourage students to predict the answers before they watch the sequence.

■ Play the sequence with the sound on. Have students work alone to check their predictions and mark *True* or *False* as they watch.

■ Find out if anyone needs to view the sequence again, and replay as necessary. Then have students compare answers with a partner.

■ Check answers around the class by asking individual students to each share an answer with the class. Encourage students to give reasons or evidence from the sequence to support their answers. Ask students to correct false statements.

Answers
1) True
2) True
3) True
4) False (She knows Sam is a very responsible person.)
5) False (She says it's an old clunker.)
6) True

B ***Pair work*** Books open. Explain the task, and then play the sequence again.

■ Have students work alone to write two more statements. Then put them into pairs to take turns asking their partners if the statements are "Probably true" or "Probably false."

■ Call on selected students to read their statements to the class, and have the class call out "Probably true" or "Probably false."

6 WHAT'S YOUR OPINION?

In these activities, students give their opinions about the video characters' personalities and feelings, and then talk about the personalities of people they know.

A *Pair work* Books open. Explain the task, and review the adjectives with the class.

■ Have students work in pairs to check off the adjectives that describe the personalities and feelings of Bill, Sam, Emily, and Debbie. Then have the pairs form small groups to compare and discuss answers.

■ Go over answers by asking selected students to share one or more answers with the class. Encourage students to give reasons for their answers. Accept all answers as long as students can support them with details from the video.

Possible answers

    Bill: carefree, reassuring, relaxed
   Sam: stressed out, tense, upset, worried
 Emily: stressed out, tense, upset, worried
Debbie: reassuring, sensible

B Books open. Explain the task, and model the sample language. Then put students into pairs to take turns talking about people they know. Encourage students to give examples of their friends' behavior to support their statements.

■ After a few minutes, ask several pairs to share their statements with the class.

Optional activity

Pair work **Describing oneself** Books open or closed. Put students into pairs to take turns talking about how they feel in different situations. Write these examples on the board:

*I think I'm a sensible student because I always
   get started on assignments right away.*
*However, when I'm driving in heavy traffic, I
   feel really stressed out.*

After a few minutes, ask for volunteers to share their statements with the class. (5 minutes)

 *Follow-up*

7 WHAT'S YOUR ADVICE?

In these extension activities, students have the opportunity to extend the language of the unit by reading people's predicaments and thinking of possible solutions to the predicaments. They also have a chance to express what they would do in such predicaments.

A Books closed. Ask students, "Have you ever visited a chat room or discussion on the Internet?" If students answer "Yes," ask for volunteers to talk about the kinds of chat rooms they visit and what they find interesting about them. If no students have visited a chat room, ask, "Why do you think Internet users spend time in chat rooms online?" Accept all answers.

■ Books open. Explain the task, and give students time to read the three predicaments. Circulate to provide help with vocabulary as needed.

B *Pair work* Books open. Explain the task, and put students into pairs to take turns giving advice for each predicament. Circulate to provide help as needed.

■ When students have finished, ask for volunteers to present their pairs' advice to the class and what they would have done. Ask for a volunteer to record the advice for each predicament on the board. Finally, ask the class to vote for the best advice for each predicament.

 *Language close-up*

8 WHAT DID THEY SAY?

This cloze activity has students focus on specific language used in conversation between Bill and Sam at the beginning of the sequence.

■ Books open. Have students, working individually or in pairs, read the conversation and fill in as many blanks as they can before watching the sequence.

(procedure continues on next page)

- Play this segment of the sequence through once while students work alone to fill in the missing words and check their predictions.

- Ask if anyone needs to watch the video again, and replay as necessary.

- Check answers around the class, and replay the segment as needed.

- Model the conversation or, if you wish, lead a choral or individual repetition of it. Then put students into pairs to practice the conversation.

Answers

Sam: We **shouldn't have spent** so much time at that gift shop.

Bill: Ah, I did the **right** thing. The top of the wedding **cake** is everything! Besides, this **shortcut** will get us **there** with time to **spare**

Sam: I still think we **should have stayed** on Highway 41. Did you **remember** the ring? Bill, you did not **forget** it?

Bill: **Relax**. It's right here. What time does the **ceremony** begin?

Sam: **Three o'clock**.

Bill: And **what time** is it now?

Sam: It's **one-thirty**.

Bill: Good. We have **plenty** of time.

Sam: Yeah, but we have to be there an hour **early** for pictures. That only gives us **half** an **hour**.

Bill: **Trust** me. We're almost there.

Sam: Except for that **"Road Closed"** sign ahead!

9 PAST MODALS FOR OPINIONS AND ADVICE

In these activities, students use past modal expressions with *should have, could have,* and *would have,* the grammatical focus of the unit, to say what Bill and Sam should have done differently, and to talk about what they themselves would have done in similar situations.

A Books open. Explain the task, and read the example sentence to the class. Then have students work alone to write their sentences.

- Circulate to help and check for accuracy. Then have students take turns reading their sentences to a partner.

- Ask selected students to share one or more of their sentences with the class.

Possible answers

1) He could have borrowed a newer car.
2) They should have left the house earlier. / They could have bought it the day before.
3) They should have stayed on Highway 41. / They could have looked at a map.
4) He should have had his car fixed.
5) They could have taken pictures after the wedding.
6) They should have called Emily to let her know what was happening.

B *Pair work* Books open. Explain the task, and lead students through the two situations. Be sure students understand that they must use *would have* in their responses.

- Put students into pairs to take turns talking about what they would have done in the four situations. Circulate to help with vocabulary and check fluency.

- Call on selected pairs to share their responses with the class.

Optional activity

Group work **Advice for different situations**
Books closed. Put students into groups of three or four. Write the following situations on the board:

1) *I forgot my best friend's birthday, and now she's mad at me.*
2) *I can't turn in my homework because I left it at home.*
3) *I overslept again and was late for work. Now my boss is mad at me.*

Have students choose one or more of the situations to discuss. Tell students to talk about what the person *should have, shouldn't have,* or *could have* done in each situation and what they themselves *would have* done. Tell students to select someone in each group to record the group's ideas. When the activity is finished, have someone from each group read their group's ideas. (15 minutes)

14 Behind the scenes in TV news

Topic/function: TV news; describing how something is made

Grammar: The passive to describe process

Summary

This documentary sequence shows how a TV news program is produced and describes the duties and responsibilities of people who work at the KMSP-TV news station. Alan Beck, the associate news director, is the person in charge of daily operations. He decides which stories to cover and which reporters will cover them, and allocates time and resources to the stories. He talks about the team effort that is necessary to produce the news. The assignment editor, Keith Brown, explains how he gathers information and story ideas. Rod Wermager, the photographer, and Vince Irby, the reporter, talk about how they collaborate on a story: The reporter gathers information and writes a script, and the photographer shoots the pictures and records the sound to accompany the story. The producer, Carrie Hoerrmann, is the manager of the newscast. She decides which stories to air, proofreads and edits them, and decides when they will be shown and how they will be presented. Leo Hofmeister, the director, is the person in charge of the control room. He coordinates the efforts of the technical staff to get the newscast on the air. He explains that directing the news is exciting because it is live. Robyne Robinson, an anchor, agrees. Her job includes listening to and watching as much news as she can, and creating scripts with the rest of the news team. We see a clip of the KMSP coverage of the Minnesota State Fair. Finally, at 11:00 P.M., the newscast is over, and the crew goes home. Tomorrow, they will all work together again to produce another newscast.

Preview

1 CULTURE

The major network TV stations in the United States air newscasts several times a day. Typically, half an hour is devoted to state and local news, and half an hour to national and international news. Cable TV stations may feature longer news programs or programs devoted to a particular story of high interest. The culture preview in the Video Activity Book builds student interest in the topic by presenting information about the different news media common in North America, and specific information about television news programs.

■ Books closed. Ask, "How do you think North Americans follow the news?" Ask students to list as many different ways as they can. Accept all answers, and write them on the board.

■ Books open. Have students read the information in the culture preview silently to check their predictions. Answer any vocabulary questions.

▪ Put students into groups of three or four to discuss the questions. Call on selected students to each share some of their group's answers.

Optional activities

A *Pair work* **Talking about news media**
Books closed. Put students into pairs. Ask each pair to talk about how the news on TV is similar to and different from another type of news medium, such as radio, newspaper, magazine, or the Internet. Let each pair choose which type of news to compare, or assign a different type to each pair. Have one student in each pair take notes on their discussion. Then have pairs share their ideas with the class. (10 minutes)

(procedure continues on next page)

B *Class activity* **News survey** Books closed. Tell the class they will be conducting a survey about the news habits of class members. Write the following questions on the board:

1) How often do you watch the news on TV?
2) What's your favorite newspaper?
3) Do you ever listen to the news on the radio?
4) What part of the newspaper do you read first?

Then ask the class to brainstorm more questions related to news until you have one question for each student in the class. Tell students to choose five questions to ask their classmates. Then have students stand and circulate, asking their questions. When everyone has finished, bring the class back together and call on selected students to summarize the answers to the questions. (15 minutes)

2 VOCABULARY *Covering the news*

In this activity, students work with idioms about TV news production by using phrases to complete sentences.

■ Books open. Explain the task, and lead students through the phrases in the box. Have students work alone to complete the sentences. Then have students compare answers with a partner.

■ Check answers around the class by calling on selected students to each read a sentence aloud.

Answers
1) choose a camera angle
2) write a script
3) deliver the news
4) shoots the pictures
5) covers the news
6) pick out a sound bite

3 GUESS THE FACTS

In this activity, students prepare to watch the sequence by predicting the job duties of three people who work at a TV news station.

■ Books open. Explain the task, and have students work alone to make their predictions.

■ Call on selected students to share their predictions with the class. At this point, do not tell students which answers are correct. Explain that the answers will become clear as they continue to work with the sequence. (The answers are given in Exercise 5 of this book.)

Optional activity

Pair work **Predicting occupations** Books closed. Have students work in pairs to guess what other kinds of jobs are associated with producing a TV news program. If students do not know the English words for the job titles, they may write a short description of job duties. When pairs are done, ask for volunteers to share their answers. Accept all answers, and write them on the board. (10 minutes)

 *Watch the video*

4 GET THE PICTURE

In these activities, students watch and listen to match the people shown in the sequence with their job titles.

■ Books open. Explain the task, and lead students through the job titles and names.

■ Play the entire sequence with the sound on for students to complete the task. Have students compare answers with a partner.

■ Ask if anyone needs to watch the sequence again, and replay as needed.

■ Check answers around the class by asking, "What does Alan Beck do?" and having volunteers answer, "He is the associate news director," etc.

Answers (from left to right)
Alan Beck: associate news director
Keith Brown: assignment editor
Rod Wermager: photographer

Vince Irby: reporter
Carrie Hoerrmann: producer
Leo Hofmeister: director
Robyne Robinson: anchor

5 WATCH FOR DETAILS

In this activity, students focus more closely on details in order to match the job titles from Exercise 4 to their descriptions.

A Books open. Explain the task, and lead students through the list of statements. Have students work alone to fill in as many blanks as they can before viewing the sequence.

■ Play the entire sequence with the sound on for students to check their work.

■ Ask if anyone needs to view the sequence again, and replay as necessary. Then have students compare answers with a partner.

■ Check answers around the class by calling on selected students to read the completed sentences.

Answers
1) associate news director
2) assignment editor
3) reporter
4) photographer
5) producer
6) director
7) anchor

B *Pair work* Books open. Explain the task, and point out the example language. Then have students work in pairs to describe the people.

■ Extend the exercise by having Student A ask, "Who is the person in charge of daily operations?" Student B gives the job title. After the pair has gone through each job title once, repeat the exercise, but have Student B try to answer with books closed.

Optional activities

A *Pair work* **Further details about jobs**
Books open or closed. Play the sequence with the sound on as many times as necessary, and have each student jot down one more piece of information about each job. Then put students into pairs or small groups to share their answers, or call on volunteers to share their additional information with the class. (15 minutes)

B *Pair work* **Discussing job preferences**
Books open. Have students work in pairs to take turns telling each other which of the jobs

mentioned in Exercise 5 they think they would enjoy doing, and which they would not enjoy doing. Encourage them to give reasons for their choices. (10 minutes)

Follow-up

6 WHAT'S NEWS?

In these communicative extension activities, students imagine they are assignment editors for a news station and plan a half-hour news program.

A *Pair work* Books open. Explain the task, and read through the story ideas with the class. Answer any vocabulary questions.

■ Have students work in pairs to choose which stories to cover and decide how much time to give each story. Encourage them to make notes about how they made their decisions. Students can also indicate, if they wish, in what order they would show the stories.

B *Group work* Books open. Explain the task, and put two pairs together to compare their news programs.

■ If time allows, switch pairs and repeat part B, or call on selected pairs to share their news program ideas with the class.

Optional activity

Pair work **Last week's news** Books closed. Tell the class that they should think back about the stories that were in the news in the past week, or month, if you prefer. They may think about local, national, or international news. Have students work in pairs to choose the five stories they would cover in an evening news program. They should indicate how much time they would give each story and in what order they would air the stories. If they like, they may add other details, such as whether they would include live coverage, an interview, a sound bite, etc. Encourage students to use the vocabulary from Exercise 2 in their discussions. Call on each pair to share their news coverage plan with the class. (15 minutes)

7 ROLE PLAY *And here's the news!*

In this communicative activity, students work with the topical focus of the lesson by role-playing a newscast.

Pair work Books open. Explain the task, and put students into pairs. Have each pair decide who will be the anchor and who will be the reporter.

■ Give pairs time to select their stories and practice their newscasts. Then have each pair present the newscast to the class or to several other pairs. If possible, videotape the newscasts to show in a subsequent lesson.

■ When the newscasts have all been presented, bring the class together and ask, "What was the most interesting part of preparing this newscast? the most difficult? the most enjoyable?", and let students volunteer answers.

Language close-up

8 WHAT DID THEY SAY?

This cloze activity has students focus on specific language used by the narrator and Robyne Robinson to explain the duties of a news anchor.

■ Books open. Have students work alone to fill in as many blanks as they can before watching the sequence. Then have students compare predictions in pairs.

■ Play this segment of the sequence through once, and have students work alone to check their predictions and fill in the blanks as they watch.

■ Have students compare answers with a partner. Then ask if anyone needs to watch the video again, and replay as necessary.

■ Play the segment once more as a final check so that students can check their answers.

■ Check answers around the class by asking students to take turns reading sentences, or by reading the answers yourself.

■ Have students work in pairs to practice the presentation, with one student reading the narrator and the other the role of Robyne Robinson. Have students switch roles and practice again.

Answers

Narrator: The anchors are the **people** viewers see **delivering** the news. At this **station**, there are **two**: a man and a woman. Robyne Robinson is one of the **anchors**.

Robyne: **Every** anchor's job is **different**. But what we usually do every day is we try to **read** as much as we can, **listen** to as much **radio** as we can . . . uh . . . **watch** as much **news** on the other **stations** and on the **network** news as possible. We take that **information**, and we write **scripts** all day long with the help of **writers** and **producers** and the reporters and **photographers**.

Narrator: After the **preparation**, Robyne and her **co-anchor** are the ones who **deliver** the **news** to the **public**.

9 PASSIVE *How a Web site is designed*

In these activities, students practice both the functional and the grammatical focus of the unit by first using the passive to complete sentences about how a Web site is designed, and then putting the steps in order to explain the entire process.

A Books open. Explain the task, and read through the sentences. Explain vocabulary if necessary.

■ Have students work alone to put the verbs in parentheses in their passive forms to complete the sentences. Then have students compare answers with a partner.

■ Check answers around the class by having selected students read aloud one sentence at a time.

Answers
is designed, viewed
is given
is tested, shown
is put online, be maintained
are discussed, be made
is built

B *Pair work* Books open. Explain the task, and
have students work in pairs to put the sentences
in order.

■ Check answers around the class before having
students describe the entire process.

■ After students have made any necessary
corrections, tell pairs to take turns describing
the entire process.

Answers
2) A prototype is designed by the developers and
   (is) viewed by the client.
3) Approval is given by the client to proceed with
   the project.
5) The Web site is tested and then (is) shown to
   the client for final approval.
6) The finished Web site is put online and may
   be maintained by the developer or the client.
1) Ideas for the Web site are discussed by the
   client and the Web developer, and decisions
   about content have to be made.
4) The Web site is built by the software team.

First, ideas for the Web site are discussed by the
client and the Web developer, and decisions
about content have to be made. Next, a prototype
is designed by the developers and viewed by the
client. Then approval is given by the client to
proceed with the project. After that, the Web site
is built by the software team. Next, the Web site
is tested and then shown to the client. Finally,
the finished Web site is put online and may be
maintained by the developer or the client.

Optional activity

Pair work **Describing a process** Books closed.
Have students work in pairs to think of a simple
process and then write down the steps needed to
complete that process. Encourage students to use
the passive tense where possible. When the class
has finished, have each pair read their sentences
aloud to the class. Have students try to identify
what process is being described. (15 minutes)

Environment or entertainment? A town debates.

Topic/function: Controversy in a town; talking about town rules

Grammar: Passive modals

Summary

This documentary sequence opens with reporter Adam Whisner standing on the site of a proposed amphitheater in the town of Burnsville, Minnesota. The area, a former garbage dump, is located on the bank of a river. The proposed amphitheater would seat nearly 20,000 people and would bring live outdoor entertainment, such as rock concerts, operas, and symphonies, to the area. The developers would pay for the cleanup of the former dump site. However, the project site is right next to a national wildlife refuge, and naturalists are concerned that the noise from shows would disturb the wildlife. Residents of homes near the proposed project are afraid of the increased noise and traffic that the amphitheater might bring. Adam Whisner interviews a number of Burnsville residents, including a wildlife biologist, the Burnsville city manager, nearby homeowners, the mayor of Burnsville, and ordinary citizens, to see whether they support or oppose the construction of the amphitheater, and why. Those who support the project talk about the reclamation of the former dump, the revenue the project would bring to the city, and the appeal of the culture and entertainment the amphitheater could bring. Those who oppose the project worry about the impact on the wildlife refuge, the nearby homes, and whether rock concerts would attract undesirable crowds. Adam Whisner closes by asking the viewers, who have heard both sides, whether they think the amphitheater should be built.

1 CULTURE

Towns considering development projects must weigh advantages and disadvantages before reaching a decision. They must examine whether increased revenue and recreational opportunities for the town will be offset by a negative impact on the environment and the quality of life of its citizens. The culture preview in the Video Activity Book raises student awareness of how towns reach decisions about projects such as the construction of the Burnsville Amphitheater.

■ Books closed. Ask, "How do you think decisions are made in small towns in the United States?" Accept all answers.

■ Books open. Have students read the information in the culture preview silently. Answer any vocabulary questions. Ask, "What did you learn about decision-making in small towns in the United States? Did any information surprise you?"

■ Put students into groups of three or four to discuss the questions. Then call on selected students to each share some of their group's answers.

Optional activity

Group work **Decision-making** Books closed. Write the following questions on the board:

1) *What are some different ways that decisions can be made in a group? List as many ways as you can.*

2) *What ways for making decisions are most appropriate for a married couple? a family with small children? a family with teenagers? a high school classroom? a sports team? a club?*

Form new groups of four to five students to discuss the questions. When groups have finished discussing, call on each group to share their ideas about the ways decisions can be made, and write these on the board. Then have each group choose one situation and tell what kind of decision-making style they think would be best for that situation, and why. (15 minutes)

2 VOCABULARY *Describing locations*

In these activities, students work with vocabulary for describing locations by first matching descriptions to illustrations of different locations and then by brainstorming additional descriptions for each location.

A Books open. Explain the task, and lead students through the vocabulary box and the illustrations.

■ Have students work alone to write words under the pictures they describe. Do not go over answers until students have completed part B.

B *Pair work* Have students work in pairs to compare their answers and think of additional words.

■ Call on selected pairs to share their answers. If pairs have different answers, encourage them to explain their choices; there are several possibilities for each picture. Write any new vocabulary words on the board.

Possible answers
garbage dump
dirty, polluted

suburb
attractive, serene

amphitheater
entertaining, noisy

wildlife refuge
attractive, natural, serene

riverfront
attractive, natural, serene

downtown
polluted, congested, entertaining, noisy

Optional activity

Pair work **Additional locations** Books open. Have students work in pairs to list one additional place that could be described by each vocabulary word. Then write each vocabulary word on the board, and call on pairs to share their places. Write each new location on the board. (10 minutes)

3 GUESS THE FACTS

In this activity, students make predictions about the arguments for and against the construction of an amphitheater in Burnsville, Minnesota.

■ Books open. Have students work alone or with a partner to make their predictions.

■ Have students compare predictions with a partner or another pair.

■ Call on selected students to share their predictions with the class. At this point, do not tell students which answers are correct, but explain that the answers will become clear as they continue to work with the sequence. (The answers are given in Exercise 4 of this book.)

Optional activity

Class activity **Predicting supporters and opposers of the amphitheater** Books closed. Tell the class that the video sequence features several people who support and several people who do not support the construction of the amphitheater. Play the entire sequence with the sound off. When students see a person (other than the reporter), they should raise their hands if they think the person supports the construction of the amphitheater. Do not tell students whether they are correct, but explain that the answers will become clear when they complete Exercise 4. (10 minutes)

 **Watch the video**

4 GET THE PICTURE

In this activity, students watch and listen to the sequence in order to determine who supports and who does not support the construction of the amphitheater.

▪ Books open. Explain the task, and give students a few moments to study the pictures.

▪ Play the entire sequence with the sound on so that students can check whether the people are for or against the amphitheater. Have students compare answers with a partner.

▪ Find out if anyone needs to watch the sequence again, and replay as needed.

▪ Ask students to compare answers with a partner, and then check answers around the class.

Answers
1) Against
2) For
3) Against
4) Against
5) For
6) For

5 WHO SAID WHAT?

In this activity, students watch and listen more closely to determine who said certain things in the sequence.

▪ Books open. Explain the task, and lead students through the list of statements.

▪ Play the entire sequence with the sound on. Have students complete the task as they watch and then compare answers with a partner.

▪ Ask if anyone needs to view the sequence again, and replay as necessary. Then check answers around the class.

Answers
5) "The amphitheater project . . . will allow us to . . . begin the cleanup of the riverfront so that our citizens can access the river."
2) "There isn't any indication that it's going to have a negative impact on the wildlife in the area."
1) "I'd prefer to see the area incorporated either into the national wildlife refuge system or be left as a natural area."
3) "So I think basically it's a . . . it's a bad plan and a bad idea."
6) "So if it means bringing in more revenue and obviously more culture to this area, then I'm all for it – definitely."
4) "In my opinion, it's going to create enormous problems with traffic."

Optional activity

Group work **Deciding for or against the amphitheater** Books open. Have students work in groups of three or five to discuss the arguments for and against building the amphitheater. The group should try to reach an agreement by consensus, but if they cannot, they should take a straight vote. Have each group report whether they voted for or against the amphitheater, and what they thought the strongest arguments were. (15 minutes)

6 GUESSING MEANING FROM CONTEXT

In this activity, students use context clues to figure out the meaning of words used in the sequence.

▪Books open. Explain the task, and read the statements with the class. Remind students to use clues in other parts of the sentence to figure out the meaning of the underlined words.

▪Have students work alone to make their guesses.

▪ Put students into pairs to compare their answers. Encourage them to point out to their partners which words in the sentences they used as clues.

- Check answers around the class.

Answers
1) In addition
2) disagreement
3) safe place
4) effect
5) happening from time to time

Follow-up

7 FOR OR AGAINST

In these extension activities, students practice giving opinions for and against the construction of a golf course.

A Books open. Point to the picture, and ask, "What do you see in this picture?"

- Explain the task, and point out the chart. Then have students work individually to list arguments for and against the golf course.

B *Group work* Books open. Explain the task, and read the example language.

- Have students work in groups of four to discuss reasons for and against the building of the golf course. Tell students they must reach a decision at the end of their discussion.

- Have a volunteer from each group explain their decision and how they reached it. Then take a class poll. Ask, "What were the most compelling arguments?"

Optional activities

A *Group work* **A development project**
Books closed. Tell the class that there are two proposals for the town that they live in: 1) to build a nuclear power plant 25 kilometers outside of town; 2) to build a dam on a nearby river for hydroelectric power. Have students work in groups of four, and choose one of the proposals to discuss. After they have given arguments for and against the proposal, they should reach a decision about whether to go ahead with the project. Call on groups to explain their decisions and how they reached them. (15 minutes)

B *Group work* **A reporter's interviews**
Books open. Have students work in groups of three. Then have them choose one of the situations from Optional activity A above. In each group, one person plays a TV news reporter, one plays a citizen who supports the project, and the third plays a citizen who opposes the project. The reporter interviews the two citizens and asks for their opinions for and against the project. Give groups time to practice their interviews, and then have groups present their interviews to the class. (15 minutes)

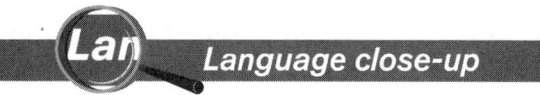
Language close-up

8 WHAT DID HE SAY?

This cloze activity has students focus on specific language used by reporter Adam Whisner to explain the controversy surrounding the construction of the Burnsville Amphitheater.

- Books open. Have students work alone to fill in as many blanks as they can before watching the sequence. Then have students compare predictions in pairs.

- Play this segment of the sequence through once, and have students work alone to check their predictions and fill in the blanks as they watch.

- Have students compare answers with a partner. Then ask if anyone needs to watch the video again, and replay as necessary.

- Play the segment once more as a final check so that students can check their answers.

- Check answers around the class by asking students to take turns reading sentences, or by reading the answers yourself.

Answers
Narrator: Hi. I'm Adam Whisner, and I'm standing on the **site** of the **controversial** project, the Burnsville Amphitheater. Burnsville is a **suburb** of Minneapolis, Minnesota, and it's **located** on the **bank** of an important river that flows through the

(answers continue on next page)

area. **According to** its supporters, the amphitheater is an **opportunity** to turn a little-used piece of land into an **attractive** outdoor **entertainment** center. It would seat almost 20,000 people and **provide** a new source of **revenue** for the city. On top of that, the city would not have to **finance** an environmental cleanup of the former **dump site**. That would be **paid** for by the **developers**. It seems like a good idea, **doesn't it**? So what's the controversy?

9 *PASSIVE MODALS* *Talking about town rules*

In these activities, students practice both the functional and the grammatical focus of the unit by using subject and object gerunds to describe jobs.

■ Books open. Explain the task, and read through the town rules. Point out the modals in the box and the example language. Then have students work individually to rewrite the town rules.

■ Check answers around the class by having selected students read aloud one sentence at a time. Encourage students with different answers to call them out.

Possible answers
1) Cars should be allowed to park on the streets overnight.
2) Cell phones ought to be banned in theaters.
3) Children should be allowed to be outside after 10:00 P.M.
4) People mustn't be permitted to smoke in libraries.
5) Dogs should be required to be on leashes at all times.
6) Homeowners have got to be required to keep their lawns mowed and yards neat.

Optional activity

Pair work **School rules** Books open or closed. Have students work in pairs to compare answers and then write a list of rules for the school they attend or where they are studying English now. They may choose to write about rules that really exist or to invent their own rules. Encourage students to use a variety of modals, both positive and negative. When students have finished, have a volunteer from each pair read their rules to the class. Have the class vote on which rules are necessary and which are a good idea. (15 minutes)

16 The ultimate challenge

Topics/function: Expeditions; Antarctica; talking about challenges

Grammar: Complex noun phrases with gerunds

Summary

This documentary sequence tells the story of the expedition of four women – Ann Bancroft, Sue Giller, Anne Dal-Vera, and Sunniva Sorby – who attempted to cross the continent of Antarctica completely under their own power, without relying on machines, dogs, or men. Through interviews with the women and actual footage from their journey, we learn how they raised the funds for their trip through contributions from schoolchildren, how they planned and prepared for their trek, and what adventures they had during their expedition. The four women began in Punta Arenas, Chile, where they were delayed for nine days by bad weather. When they arrived on the continent of Antarctica, they had to make up for the lost time by attempting to cover ten miles each day. The women discuss their challenges and how they planned to meet them. They also documented some of the unexpected problems that occurred: a respiratory infection, tendinitis, and a sprained ankle. When their morale was low, a military supply plane flew overhead and dropped a surprise package for the women, containing some gifts and words of encouragement from a group of scientists and military personnel. This gave the women the mental strength they needed to reach the South Pole. Because of injuries to some team members and the lost time, the four women decided not to continue across the continent but to end the expedition with their successful arrival at the Pole. As the sequence ends, we learn of Ann's future plans to try again with a new partner to become the first women to cross the entire Antarctic continent under their own power.

Preview

1 CULTURE

This sequence provides an example of how challenges can enrich people's lives, and what skills and strengths people need to meet those challenges. The culture preview in the Video Activity Book engages students' interest in the topic by raising their awareness of the role that challenges play in their own and other people's lives.

■ Books closed. Ask, "What kinds of challenges do people experience in their lives? What kinds of challenges do people look for?" Accept all answers.

■ Books open. Have students read the information in the culture preview silently. Answer any vocabulary questions.

■ Put students into groups of three or four to discuss the questions. Call on selected students to each share some of their group's answers.

2 VOCABULARY *Synonyms*

In these activities, students work with vocabulary to talk about an expedition by matching synonyms to words in four different categories, and then they discuss topics related to the four categories.

A *Pair work* Books open. Explain the task, and lead students through the box with vocabulary words and the chart. If necessary, explain the word *synonym* (a word that has the same or a similar meaning to another word).

■ Have students work in pairs to put the vocabulary words into the chart.

■ Check answers around the class by asking, for example, "What words are synonyms for *goal*?"

(procedure continues on next page)

Answers

Goal	Expedition	Equipment	Mental strength
dream	mission	gear	fortitude
plan	journey	supplies	morale
vision	undertaking	machines	spirits

B Books open. Have students work with a partner to discuss the topics. Encourage students to use as many words as they can from the chart in part A.

▪ Call on students to share their partners' answers to one of the discussion topics with the class.

---

3 GUESS THE FACTS

In this activity, students use visual information to make a prediction about the nature of the expedition featured in the sequence.

▪ Books open. Have students look at the picture, and explain the task.

▪ Check predictions around the class by asking, "Who thinks these four women are planning to compete in a skiing competition?", etc., and have students raise their hands to indicate their prediction.

▪ Tell students, "This sequence is about four women who are planning to cross Antarctica on foot." Ask, "What do you know about Antarctica?" and have students volunteer information. Accept all answers.

▪ Read the following information about Antarctica to the class. (This information does not appear in the Video Activity Book or the video sequence.)

"Antarctica is the fifth largest continent on the earth. It is about one and a half times as large as the United States. It is the coldest, windiest, highest (on average), and driest continent. It is ninety-eight percent ice and two percent barren rock. Even in the warmest part of the year – the southern hemisphere summer of December to February – temperatures average below freezing, and strong winds and blizzards add to the harsh climate. Antarctica has no permanent population, but researchers and scientists number about 1,000 in the winter and about 4,000 in the summer. Scientists study land and

ocean animals, polar weather and conditions, and issues surrounding the hole in the ozone layer. In the 1998–1999 summer, 10,013 tourists visited Antarctica on cruise ships and yachts. The first person to cross the entire continent of Antarctica was Sir Edmund Hillary (also the first person to climb Mt. Everest), who made the trip in 1958 using motorized sleds."

Optional activity

Pair work **Predicting challenges** Books closed. Have students work in pairs to make a list of challenges they think the four women will face as they attempt to cross Antarctica on foot. Call on pairs to share their predictions with the class. (10 minutes)

 *Watch the video*

4 GET THE PICTURE

In this activity, students watch and listen to put the events of the women's expedition in order.

▪ Books open. Explain the task, and lead students through the list of events. Encourage students to predict as many answers as they can before watching the sequence, and have students compare predictions with a partner.

▪ Play the entire sequence with the sound on so that students can check and revise their predictions.

▪ Find out if anyone needs to watch the sequence again, and replay as needed.

▪ Ask students to compare answers with a partner, and then check answers around the class.

Answers
1) Ann's dream was to cross Antarctica without dogs, machines, or men.
2) Ann and her team were able to raise funds by asking schools for donations.
3) In Chile, bad weather delayed their departure for nine days.
4) To keep on schedule, the team had to travel at least ten miles a day.
5) Sunniva came down with a respiratory infection.

6) Sunniva sprained her ankle.

7) A military supply plane dropped an unexpected package for the team.

8) The four women were able to reach the South Pole.

9) The women decided to end their adventure with their arrival at the South Pole.

Optional activities

A *Pair work* **Telling the story of the expedition** Books open. Have students work in pairs to take turns telling the story of the expedition from beginning to end. Have students use words like *first, next, then, after that,* and *finally.* (5 minutes)

B *Group work* **Additional events** Books open. Have students watch the entire sequence again with the sound on, and ask each student to write two more events in the expedition. Tell students to mark in their books where in the list of events in Exercise 4 their additional events occurred. Then put students into groups of three, and have them take turns telling each other their additional events. The other group members predict where in the sequence in Exercise 4 the new events occurred. When all group members have finished telling their events, play the sequence again with the sound on for students to check their predictions. (15 minutes)

5 WATCH FOR DETAILS

In these activities, students focus more closely on details in order to gather information about each of the four women on the expedition, and then they share this information with a partner.

A Books open. Explain the task, and give students time to look at the photographs of the four women.

■ Play the entire sequence with the sound on, and have students write their information under each picture.

■ Ask if anyone needs to view the sequence again, and replay as necessary. Do not go over the answers until students have finished part B.

B *Pair work* Have students work in pairs to compare information. If any students have contradictory information, play the sequence again.

■ Check answers around the class. Several different answers are possible for each woman.

Possible answers

Ann Bancroft: the expedition leader; a former teacher; from St. Paul, Minnesota

Sue Giller: a computer programmer and outdoor enthusiast; from Boulder, Colorado; the expedition's navigator

Anne Dal-Vera: from Colorado; had extensive winter camping experience; the team's strongest skier

Sunniva Sorby: from San Diego, California; a winter-camping enthusiast; had extensive wilderness-trekking experience

Optional activity

Pair work **Memory quiz** Books open and closed. Have students work in pairs. Tell students that they will take turns asking their partners about the expedition. Student A keeps the book open and asks, "Who was the expedition leader?", etc. Student B tries to answer with the book closed. Then have students switch roles and repeat the activity. (5 minutes)

6 WHAT'S YOUR OPINION?

In these activities, students personalize the information in the sequence by ranking different challenges of the Antarctic expedition in order of difficulty and then by sharing their opinions with a partner.

A Books open. Explain the task, and lead students through the phrases.

■ Have students work individually to make their rankings. Give students time to think of reasons for their rankings. Suggest that they make a few notes for their discussion.

B *Pair work* Put students into pairs to discuss their rankings and to talk about any additional challenges they can think of.

(see next page for an optional activity)

■ Call on selected students to say which aspect they would find the most challenging and which the least challenging. Ask volunteers to share any additional challenges they thought of.

Optional activity

Group work **Ann Bancroft's next challenge**
Remind the class that the end of the sequence talks about Ann Bancroft's plan to try again to cross Antarctica on foot – this time with a single partner, Liv Arnesen. Read the following to the class:

"For her next trip, Ann teamed up with another former schoolteacher, Liv Arnesen from Norway. Before she left, she said, 'My motivation often comes from the students and people that follow the adventure. On my last expedition to Antarctica, thoughts of kids all over the nation following us inspired me on tough days to stay at it. I know this will be a strong force on this upcoming crossing. I am also living my dream and doing what I feel I was meant to do. It is totally energizing to step out each day living a dream.' Liv commented, 'Our upcoming expedition . . . can give [the] message to thousands of kids and adults that believing in your dream will make your life into an adventure. And it's not about Antarctica, but being faithful to yourself.' The two women pulled sleds of 250 pounds (114 kg), and traveled 2,400 miles (3,850 km). When wind conditions were right, Ann and Liv were pulled forward on their skis by giant kites. This time, the women were successful. They completed their expedition on February 18, 2001."

Write these discussion questions on the board:

1) *What kind of challenges do you think Ann and Liv faced that might have been different from the ones that the four women in the sequence faced?*
2) *What kinds of challenges do you think Ann Bancroft and the other women might undertake in the future?*

Have students work in groups of three or four to discuss the questions. Then call on selected students from each group to share their group's ideas. (*Note:* Further information and details about Ann Bancroft's expeditions

and future plans can be found at www.yourexpedition.com.) (15 minutes)

Follow-up

7 PLANNING AN EXPEDITION

In these communicative activities, students work with a partner to plan an imaginary expedition and then share their plans in a group.

A *Pair work* Books open. Explain the task, and go over the chart. Then put students into pairs to plan their expeditions. Circulate to help with vocabulary.

B *Group work* Books open. Put two or three pairs together, and have pairs take turns describing their expeditions. Have listeners ask questions and make comments.

Optional activity

Pair work **An interview** Books closed. Have students work with their partners from part A. This time, one student will play a reporter and the other will play the leader of the expedition. Tell students to imagine that the expedition has been completed. The reporter will ask questions about how the trip went, what was challenging, etc. The expedition leader will answer the questions. Have pairs practice their interviews several times, and then have pairs present their interviews to the class. (15 minutes)

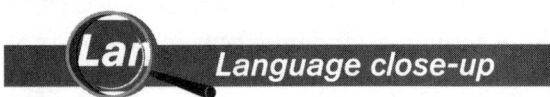
Language close-up

8 WHAT DID THEY SAY?

This cloze activity has students focus on specific language used by the narrator and Ann Bancroft to explain the plan and preparation for the expedition.

■ Books open. Have students work alone to fill in as many blanks as they can before watching the sequence. Then have students compare predictions in pairs.

■ Play this segment of the sequence through once, and have students work alone to check their predictions and fill in the blanks as they watch.

- Have students compare answers with a partner. Then ask if anyone needs to watch the video again, and replay as necessary.

- Play the segment once more as a final check so that students can check their answers.

- Check answers around the class by asking students to take turns reading sentences, or by reading the answers yourself.

- Have students work in pairs to read the commentaries: Student A is the narrator and Student B is Ann Bancroft. Then have students switch roles and repeat the task.

Answers

Narrator: The **plan** was first to **travel** the 975 kilometers from the **coast** of Antarctica to the South Pole. This **portion** of the **journey** would be all **uphill** and against the **wind**. The **last** 1,500 kilometers – from the South Pole to the **opposite** coast – would be **downhill** and **with** the wind. The **goal**: to reach the **other** side of the Antarctic **continent** in time to **catch** a free ride **home** on a **tourist** cruise ship.

Ann Bancroft: So we **started** the wheels **turning**, of becoming an **organization**, working on our **mission** and our **vision**.

Narrator: **Carrying out** an enormous **undertaking** like this required **months** of planning, **organizing**, training, and **fund-raising**.

---

9 COMPLEX NOUN PHRASES WITH GERUNDS *Talking about challenges*

In these activities, students practice both the functional and the grammatical focus of the unit by using complex noun phrases with gerunds to interview a partner about meeting a challenge.

A *Pair work* Books open. Explain the task, and read through the questions with the class.

- Have students work in pairs to ask and answer the questions. Make sure each student tells something about his or her challenge before the partner chooses which questions to ask. Have one student ask all of his or her questions while the partner answers. Then have students switch roles.

Possible answers

(*Note:* Answers will depend on which questions were asked and how the partner answered, but should start like below.)

1) The most physically challenging part was . . .
2) The most mentally challenging part was . . .
3) One of the rewards was . . .
4) The most dangerous aspect was . . .
5) The easiest part was . . .
6) The most surprising thing that happened was . . .
7) The most exciting event was . . .
8) The happiest moment was . . .
9) The scariest moment was . . .
10) The funniest moment was . . .

B *Group work* Books open. Put pairs together, and have students take turns telling the group about their partner's challenging experience.

- If time permits, call on selected students to each share their partner's challenging experience with the class.

Optional activity

Pair work **Writing about the imaginary expedition** Have students work with the same partner with whom they planned an expedition in Exercise 7. Have students answer five of the questions from Exercise 9 about their imaginary expeditions. Put two pairs together to share their sentences, or have one student from each pair read the sentences aloud to the class.
(10 minutes)

1 Dream Date

A young woman chooses one of three men for her date on a dating game show.

Host: Hello, everyone, and welcome to *Dream Date,* the game where one lucky woman gets to choose her perfect date. I'm your host, Lucky Chance. Now, let's meet our first contestant.

Announcer: Lucky, meet Sarah Hawkins, a social studies teacher from Ames, Iowa.

Host: Hello, Sarah, and welcome to *Dream Date.*

Sarah: Hi, Lucky. It's great to be here.

Host: Now, Sarah, before we bring out our three bachelors, why don't you tell us something about yourself?

Sarah: Well, I'm twenty-eight years old. I'm interested in American history and government. I . . . I enjoy talking about politics, literature, the arts . . . about a lot of things, really.

Host: And what qualities do you look for in a guy?

Sarah: Well, I like someone who's honest and straightforward, and someone who's a good conversationalist. Also, I like it when someone is more interested in other people than he is in himself. I think that's really important.

Host: Well, those are all good qualities. Is there anything you *don't* like in a guy?

Sarah: Well, I can't stand it when a guy talks about himself all the time. That's something that really bothers me.

Host: Well, Sarah, now that we know a little about you, why don't you have a seat? And let's bring out our three bachelors so you can choose your "dream date."

• • •

Host: Welcome, gentlemen. It's good to have you with us. Would each of you like to say hello to Sarah? Bachelor Number 1.

Bachelor 1: Yo, Sarah!

Host: Bachelor Number 2.

Bachelor 2: Hi, Sarah.

Host: And Bachelor Number 3.

Bachelor 3: Hello, Sarah!

Host: Thank you, bachelors. OK, Sarah, let's get started. Go ahead and ask your first question. And remember, you have to make your choice based on the answers you receive.

Sarah: OK. Bachelor Number 1. If you were out with your friends and then showed up late for our first date, what excuse would you give when you arrived?

Bachelor 1: Well, I'd be too embarrassed to tell you the truth, so I'd probably say that I had car trouble or got stuck in traffic or something.

Sarah: OK. Bachelor Number 2, same question.

Bachelor 2: Well, it really bothers me when people lie – and I wouldn't want to start our relationship on a lie – so I would tell you the truth, and I'd hope you'd be generous enough to forgive me.

Sarah: Bachelor Number 3?

Bachelor 3: Well, that's happened on other dates, as a matter of fact. I'd probably be honest with you and tell you what I tell everyone: "I'm sorry, but, uh, it's hard to divide my time among so many people!"

Sarah: Oh, really? OK. Uh, Bachelor Number 1, what's your idea of the ideal date?

Bachelor 1: Well, I think getting together with a bunch of my friends, having a barbecue, and heading out to a football game. Yeah, that would be a great date.

Sarah: OK. Uh, Bachelor Number 3, same question.

Bachelor 3: For me, I think I would take you to my favorite nightclub where everybody knows me.

Sarah: And how about you, Number 2? What's your idea of the perfect date?

Bachelor 2: I'd take you out to a nice dinner. That way you could relax and enjoy the evening, and we could get to know each other better.

Sarah: Great. OK. Uh, Bachelor Number 2, tell me two things about yourself: one positive and one negative.

Bachelor 2: Well, let's see. I . . . I think I'm a pretty good friend, and people trust me. Uh, negative . . . I'm very direct, and that sometimes upsets people.

Sarah: Oh, no, that's good, Number 2. Uh, Number 3, tell me something good about yourself and something not so good.

Bachelor 3: Actually, I'm pretty good at most things I do. And something not so good. . . . I can't think of anything.

Sarah: OK. Uh, Bachelor Number 1, tell me something positive and something negative about yourself.

Bachelor 1: Well, I guess I'm pretty easygoing. That's something good about me. Something bad. Well, I guess I'm not very ambitious. I mean, I don't care if I make a lot of money or save the world. I just like watching sports with my friends.

Host: OK, Sarah. Let's have a few final questions, and then you'll have to make your choice.

Sarah: OK. Uh, Bachelor Number 1, finish this sentence: "I can't stand it when . . ."

Bachelor 1: I can't stand it when people are talking while I'm watching the football game on TV.

Sarah: OK. Uh, Bachelor Number 3, finish this sentence: "I think it's disgusting when . . ."

Bachelor 3: I think it's disgusting when I'm at an expensive restaurant and I don't get the service I deserve.

Sarah: OK. Bachelor Number 2: "It really bothers me when . . ."

Bachelor 2: It bothers me when people get mad and they get into arguments over unimportant things. I just think people should be more easygoing and treat each other better.

Host: OK, Sarah. We're out of time. Now, I'm going to ask you to make a choice based on the answers you received. Who will that special date be with? Will it be Bachelor Number 1, . . . Number 2, . . . or Number 3?

Sarah: Well, they all sounded really nice, but I think I'm going to choose Bachelor Number 2.

Host: Great! OK. Was there any specific reason?

Sarah: Oh, well, like I said, they all sounded like great guys, but I liked what Number 2 said about being late for a date and being able to trust him. I appreciate it when people are honest with me. Also, he seemed interested in doing things to please me and not just himself.

Host: Well, before we meet your "dream date," let's say hello to the two men you didn't choose.

Announcer: Sarah, Bachelor Number 1 is twenty-nine years old. He's a former college football star from Pocatello, Idaho. He says he loves playing or watching almost every kind of sport. Sarah, meet Kevin Banks.

Sarah: Hi.

Bachelor 1: See you.

Announcer: Bachelor Number 3 is a thirty-year-old actor from Los Angeles. He says everyone should recognize him from his role on the soap opera *My World*. Sarah, meet Chip Billings.

Bachelor 3: Sarah.

Sarah: Chip.

Bachelor 3: Your loss!

Announcer: And finally, your choice: Bachelor Number 2. He comes from your own hometown of Ames, Iowa. In his free time, he enjoys reading and surfing the Internet. Sarah, meet Jim Chandler.

Sarah: Jim Chandler? Oh, my gosh! Jim, it's you? Oh, my gosh! We went to high school together.

Jim: Sarah Hawkins? I don't believe it! I thought you moved back East after graduation.

Sarah: And I thought you went to . . .

Host: Well, once again, one lucky woman finds her "dream date." That's our show. I'm Lucky Chance, hoping all your dates are "dream dates."

2 Urban artist

A muralist talks about his career and what motivates his painting.

Narrator: José Curbelo is an urban muralist from Minneapolis, Minnesota. Together with his team of aspiring young artists, he creates murals in inner-city neighborhoods.

José Curbelo: I love working with people. I love doing my own thing, I love writing my own paycheck, and I like to be involved in the life of the . . . the community. Working on murals, you're at one place – at one street corner – for twelve, fourteen hours a day, and you see everything that goes on.

Narrator: José feels his murals can provide color and a sense of hope and pride in an environment that can sometimes be dull and boring.

José Curbelo: In my opinion, the murals are necessary to the life of a community, because ever since way back when – hundreds of thousands of years ago – people have expressed themselves in a public way. Whether for spiritual reasons or for political reasons, or just to be creative, people have expressed themselves on walls, and I wouldn't be doing what I'm doing now if . . . you know, people didn't write on caves . . . you know, thousands of years ago or write on subway trains in the seventies.

Narrator: José's interest in art began at an early age. At thirteen, he got involved in his first mural project. From then on, mural painting became a passion.

José Curbelo: It's something that comes from . . . from your heart and comes from your own creativity. That's the importance of it.

Narrator: After high school, with some friends, José started his own mural-painting business called "Creative Energy Murals." Shortly after that, he realized he needed to learn more about how to use his art as a positive force in the community, so he attended a special program in urban art at a college in California. Now he's back home, doing what he loves. José says that even though some of his friends make more money than he does, his job provides other compensations.

José Curbelo: I may not earn as much money as someone working for a corporation, but I think the rewards in what I get out of my job is . . . is worth way more than . . . than money. I enjoy just being out there doing something good, painting, making public space a little bit more beautiful and more human.

Narrator: Another enjoyable part of José's job is supervising and guiding the young people he has selected to be on his team.

José Curbelo: It's fun. It's fun. I like working with . . . uh . . . with kids. I'm just a kid myself. I mean, the workers who are working on the project now are about fourteen to eighteen, and I'm only twenty-two. It's like a friend, but you're kind of like a boss, too, and it's a fine line. So, I mean, you just have to make sure that . . . uh . . . that people stay focused and stay committed to what the project is, which is painting a mural.

Narrator: But there's more to the job of an urban artist than just painting pictures. For each project, a location has to be found, permission must be obtained, and someone must be convinced to provide financing.

José Curbelo: First, what we do is we go out looking for a wall, or maybe we already know the wall because we see it every day. And then we just sit down and plan and draw and figure out ideas for what we might do. Either the business owner will pay for it; otherwise, we have to go and find funding. So we have to write applications and write grants to different organizations – with the city and arts groups – for money. And so we're competing with other people, with other groups. And that's kind of hard sometimes. And then we just sit there and wait and hope that we get . . . uh . . . that we get the money, and sometimes it comes through and sometimes it doesn't. It's kind of like a big gamble. But once we have the money, then we can buy materials, and then we set a schedule of when people are going to work and what are we going to do. What I like doing is . . . uh . . . is organizing these projects, getting everything together, and making sure that it happens in the best way possible. And then we just meet, and then we paint it. Each day it's something different. There's new problems and new situations that . . . that arise that you have to . . . you have to deal with and solve, so it's not the same old thing. Every single day is completely different. I like just beautifying where I live, you know, and just being able to drive by a place that you've painted and just have that . . . you know, that good feeling that . . . uh . . . you've helped do that. And I like the fact that somehow I'm passing something along to the kids.

Narrator: Thanks to the work of José and his team, some inner-city neighborhoods in Minneapolis are a little brighter. And residents there will be able to enjoy these colorful, inspiring murals for many years to come.

3 Kid sister

A woman asks her friend to look after her younger sister overnight.

Renee: Hello?

Abby: Renee? I am so glad you're there. I was wondering if you could help me out.

Renee: What's up?

Abby: I need to ask a big favor. My boss just called, and he wants me to go out of town this afternoon to meet with a client.

Renee: Great! You wanted to work with more clients.

Abby: Yeah. But the problem is my parents are out of town and my little sister is staying with me for the weekend.

Renee: Hmm. That *is* a problem.

Abby: Yeah, that's why I'm calling. Would you mind if she stayed with you? It would only be for tonight. I'll pick her up tomorrow morning by ten o'clock.

Renee: No, I wouldn't mind at all. But could you ask her to bring something to entertain herself while I work on my report?

Abby: Sure, no problem. Oh, this is great. You're the best friend. Is it OK if I drop her off on my way to the airport?

Renee: Uh, sure. That's fine.

• • •

Renee: Hi.

Abby: Hi, Renee. This is my sister Kathy.

Renee: Hi, Kathy.

Kathy: Hey, great apartment!

Abby: She's going through a stage. She brought her homework, and she has her CD player, as you can see. So, hopefully, she'll keep herself busy.

Renee: We'll be fine.

Abby: Oh, I've got to run. Good luck, and thanks a million, Renee.

Renee: You're welcome.

Abby: Bye.

Renee: Bye.

• • •

Renee: So, what grade are you in, Kathy?

Kathy: Eighth. Wow, you've got a lot of CDs! Would you mind if I listened to some of them?

Renee: No, go right ahead. Just be careful with them. You can do your homework on the coffee table over here.

Kathy: OK. Can I watch some TV?

Renee: Sure, that's fine. I have some of my own work to do in the kitchen. Is there anything I can get for you?

Kathy: No, I'm OK.

Renee: OK.

• • •

Renee: Kathy, would you mind turning the volume down a bit?

Kathy: What?

Renee: Would you turn the volume down?

Kathy: Oh, OK.

• • •

Kathy: I finished my math. Do you have anything to eat around here? I'm starving.

Renee: Oh, I'm sorry. I didn't know it was so late. How about a pizza? I have one in the freezer.

Kathy: What?

Renee: Pizza.

Kathy: Oh, that's OK, I guess. Do you have anything else?

Renee: Nope. Just pizza.

Kathy: Well, pizza's OK, I guess.

Renee: Good.

Kathy: Hey, nice laptop. Would you mind my using it?

Renee: Uh, I'm sorry. I still have some work to finish. Maybe later?

Kathy: OK. Is it all right if I use your phone to call one of my friends?

Renee: Sure. Why don't you use the one in the living room? I'll let you know when the pizza's ready.

Kathy: OK.

• • •

Kathy: Hi. This is Kathy. Is Allison there? . . . OK.

• • •

Renee: Kathy, the pizza's ready!

Kathy: Oh, my gosh!

Renee: Kathy?

Kathy: Did he say that? . . . So what did *you* say?

Renee: Kathy!

Kathy: I know *he* said it. But what did *you* say? . . . You didn't!

Renee: Kathy, your pizza's getting cold! . . . Ohhh!

Kathy: Oh, gee, Renee, I'm sorry. I'll pick them up.

Renee: It's all right, Kathy. Why don't you go have your pizza? I'll take care of it.

Kathy: Are you sure?

Renee: Yes! Go ahead.

Kathy: Oh, thanks, Renee. I'm starving.

• • •

Kathy: I'm tired. I think I'll get ready for bed now. Is it all right if I take a shower?

Renee: You're finished with your pizza already?

Kathy: Yeah.

Renee: Sure. Uh, there's towels on the shelf in the bathroom, and soap and shampoo are in the shower.

Kathy: OK.

Renee: Oh, and I'll put out some sheets and a pillow so you can make the couch into a bed. Would you like me to lend you a hand?

Kathy: No. I'm fine, thanks.

• • •

Renee: Good morning. You were reading *Harry Potter*?

Kathy: Oh, yeah. I loved it. I found it in your bookcase. Is it yours?

Renee: It sure is. I have the rest of the series in my bedroom.

Kathy: All of them?

Renee: Yep. . . . I'm a huge fan. I reread them all the time.

Kathy: I loved it when they snuck out to go to the magic sweet shop.

Renee: Me, too. What do you think about the part when . . . ?

• • •

Abby: Hi.

Renee: Hi, Abby. You're early.

Abby: Actually, I'm . . . I'm late. . . . It's 10:30. Kathy, are you ready to go?

Kathy: Oh, gee, Abby, I'm sorry. Renee and I were just talking about *Harry Potter*.

Renee: Yeah. We must have lost track of time.

Kathy: I'll just grab my stuff. It will only be a minute.

Abby: Huh! You two really seemed to hit it off. I haven't seen her without her headphones in a long time. How did you do it?

Renee: Well, I guess a good book can still bring people together, even if it seems like they're worlds apart.

97

4 Bigfoot lives!

Three friends go on a camping trip and one plays a practical joke.

Amy: You guys are never going to believe this! I was down at the bathhouse. I had already showered and I was brushing my teeth when this woman came in with an incredible story!

Cristina: What happened?

Amy: Well, she said that earlier tonight, just after dark, there was a Bigfoot sighting.

Beth: A what?

Amy: A Bigfoot sighting. You know, that huge half-man, half-beast that lives in the woods?

Cristina: They say he looks something like an eight-foot-tall gorilla-man. He's got huge feet. There have been sightings all over the U.S. and Canada.

Beth: Is that true?

Cristina: Of course it's not true. Bigfoot is just a story, so there's no way anybody could have seen him.

Amy: I hate to disagree, but let me tell you everything this woman said.

Cristina: All right. Go ahead. Tell us.

Amy: OK. Well, she said that this couple over on the other side of the campground had finished their dinner and they were building a fire. Suddenly, they heard a rustling from the woods and then a strange moaning sound. They could hardly believe their eyes when this huge hairy creature came and picked up a whole box of their food and carried it away through the woods.

Beth: Oh, no!

Cristina: Did they go after him?

Amy: I don't know. She didn't say.

Beth: You know what? I think this kind of talk is ridiculous, and I'm not listening anymore. There are no such things as monsters. I'm going to the bathhouse to shower and brush my teeth.

Cristina: Better take your flashlight with you. I don't think he likes the light, but if the light doesn't scare him, you can use your flashlight as a weapon!

Beth: Ha-ha, very funny.

Amy: Say, Cristina. How about toasting some marshmallows?

Cristina: Good idea. I'll go get the marshmallows.

Amy: I'll go find some sticks.

• • •

Sound: Roaarrr!

• • •

Beth: [*screams*]

• • •

Beth: Hey, Cristina, I saw him! I saw him!

Cristina: Saw who?

Beth: Bigfoot! In the woods, over there.

Cristina: Whoa, hold on. Tell me what happened.

Beth: Well, I was on the path to the bathhouse when I heard this noise like some big animal in the woods.

Cristina: Uh-huh.

Beth: And I shined my flashlight towards the noise, and I saw it.

Amy: Saw what?

Beth: Bigfoot.

Cristina: Beth thinks she just encountered Bigfoot on the path to the bathhouse.

Amy: Beth, he doesn't exist. I'm sorry I ever told that dumb story.

Cristina: Where's your flashlight?

Beth: When I heard him, I dropped it along with my towel and other stuff.

Cristina: Come on. Let's go get your stuff, and I'll show you there's nothing to be afraid of.

• • •

Beth: Oh. See? There's my stuff.

Sound: Roaarrr!

Beth: What was that? Did . . . did you hear that?

Cristina: The question is: What *is* it?

Beth: Oh, no! It's him. It's Bigfoot!

Cristina: Beth, stop it! There's no such thing as Bigfoot. It's just some animal . . . some *small* animal. . . . You head for camp. I'm going to figure out what's going on.

Beth: OK.

• • •

Beth: Amy! Hey, Amy! Did you hear it? Did you hear it?

Amy: Yeah, I did. Come over here and look at this.

• • •

Amy: Looks like whoever . . . whatever it was came pretty close to camp.

Beth: That does it. I'm leaving. I'm not staying here one minute longer than I have to.

• • •

Cristina: Hey, Beth! Come back. I think the mystery of Bigfoot is solved.

Beth: What?

Cristina: I discovered these over there in the bushes.

Beth: What? You think someone used those to make the creature?

Cristina: Exactly.

Amy: That's terrible! Why would anyone want to scare us like that?

Cristina: I was wondering that myself.

Amy: You don't think *I* did it!

Cristina: I do. First, before you told us about Bigfoot, you had already left a bearskin and tape recorder hidden in the woods. Then, when Beth left to take a shower, you went to get some sticks to toast the marshmallows. You were gone when Beth had her encounter with Bigfoot.

Amy: That was just a coincidence!

Cristina: Was it? You didn't come with us when Beth and I went to get her flashlight and things. After we left, you had plenty of time to reset the recorder and to make the footprints before we returned.

Beth: Aha! Busted!

Amy: You're pretty good, Cristina. I didn't think I'd get caught.

Beth: Amy, how could you?

Amy: Come on, guys. I was only kidding . . . just having fun. I didn't think you'd actually believe it. Forgive me?

Beth: Well, I guess. But no more practical jokes, OK?

Amy: I promise. Anyway, now everybody knows Bigfoot is just a story.

Cristina: Yeah.

Sound: Roaarrr!

Amy: Or is he?

5 Travel World

Reporters around the world ask people about cross-cultural experiences.

Chris Brooks: Hi. I'm Chris Brooks. Welcome to *Travel World*. Have you ever traveled to a country with a completely different culture? If you have, you probably know what "culture shock" is. It's a feeling of confusion you get from suddenly being in a new environment. The traditions and customs may seem strange. Expectations are different. You don't know exactly what you're supposed to do. You may even be a little bit afraid of making a mistake. In time, you get used to everything. But when you get home, you often have some interesting and perhaps humorous stories to tell about your cross-cultural experiences. Today, we're going to Latin America to meet some people who've traveled abroad and hear about their experiences crossing cultures. First, let's go to Brazil.

• • •

Chris: Ah, yes. Rio de Janeiro – that picturesque city of beautiful beaches, Carnaval, and samba. Enjoying a spectacular view of Sugar Loaf Mountain is our lucky reporter Fátima Nolan.

Fátima Nolan: Hi, Chris. I'm here in beautiful Rio de Janeiro. Like everywhere else in the world, people here like to travel abroad and have some interesting stories to tell. Let's talk with some of them.

• • •

Fátima: What's your name, and where are you from?

Camilla: My name is Camilla, and I was born in Stockholm, Sweden, but I moved to Rio when I was four, and I've lived here ever since. Two years ago, I went to Sweden, and I lived there for a year.

Fátima: What did you notice that was different?

Camilla: Well, the first thing that I noticed when I got to Sweden was how people greet each other. It was completely different. Because here in Brazil, we kiss on the cheek and they shake hands. So I went to kiss like [*kissing sounds*] and they . . . "Oh, my goodness!

What's going on?" And they felt like, "You're invading my space" or something like that. It was strange.

• • •

Fátima: What's your name, and where are you from?

Mônica: Uh, my name is Mônica, and I'm from Brazil.

Fátima: And where have you traveled?

Mônica: Uh, I went to Japan, and I lived there for six months.

Fátima: Is there anything that surprised you when you went to Japan?

Mônica: Well, you know there are a lot of earthquakes in Japan. And one thing that surprised me was that . . . uh . . . people stayed very calm during an earthquake. And I guess they are accustomed to them.

Fátima: Do you think that people would react differently here in Brazil?

Mônica: Well, I think here in Brazil if we had an earthquake, people would get very frightened and would run away.

Fátima: Hope your next cross-cultural experience is a good one. This is Fátima Nolan from Rio de Janeiro. Back to you, Chris!

Chris: Thanks, Fátima. Now, let's cross the South American continent to Lima, Peru, where our reporter, Denise Arregui, is standing by. Denise?

Denise Arregui: Thanks, Chris. We're here at the beautiful Plaza de Armas. This is a favorite spot for tourists and the people of Lima. Let's talk to some people here about their cross-cultural experiences.

• • •

Denise: Hi. What's your name, and where are you from?

Sally Hekobo: I'm Sally Hekobo. I'm from the Philippines, but I've been living here since 1986.

Denise: And what most surprised you when you came to Peru?

Sally: Uh, what most surprised me upon coming to Peru was the public display of affection, because in the Philippines couples don't kiss in public. And I feel really uncomfortable when I see these things, you know, and, uh, sometimes I feel embarrassed in such a situation. And you know, in the Philippines, when . . . whenever we . . . uh . . . we are on the streets – we are in public – it is not really acceptable to . . . to kiss in public.

• • •

Denise: Hi. What's your name, and where are you from?

Andrew Levin: My name's Andrew, and I'm from the United States.

Denise: Have you noticed any difference in the way people do things here in Peru?

Andrew: Yeah. One thing that I really notice is the public transportation system is really different. Because here the bus system is private, and so there's all these people trying to get you on their bus because the way they make money is by getting as many people as possible to get on their bus. So the whole time they're yelling, "Get on my bus! Get on my bus!" And sometimes it's not the bus that you want to be getting on.

Denise: This is Denise Arregui here in Lima, Peru. Back to you, Chris.

Chris: Thank you, Denise. Now, reporter Hilary García is standing by in Mexico, our final destination for today. What do you have for us, Hilary?

Hilary García: Thanks, Chris. I'm here in beautiful Tepoztlán, Mexico – a town that both Mexican and foreign tourists like to visit. Let's talk with a few of them about their cross-cultural experiences.

• • •

Hilary: What's your name, and where are you from?

Monie: My name is Monie, and I'm from Minnesota – from the United States.

Hilary: And how long have you been in Mexico?

Monie: I've been living in Mexico for about a year now.

Hilary: Have you noticed any cultural differences between Mexicans and Americans?

Monie: Yes, I have. I teach English, and at the school that I work at, Mexican women tend to dress more professionally: high heels, nylons, makeup, hair in perfect order. And we Americans tend to dress more casually: in jeans, tennis shoes, T-shirts.

• • •

Hilary: Hi. What's your name, and where are you from?

Delfino Valdez: My name is Delfino Valdez, and I was born in Renosa, Mexico, and now I live in the United States.

Hilary: Tell us about your cross-cultural experience.

Delfino: I am married to an American woman. And she was making me lunch one day, and she brought me a soup and a sandwich. Once I was done with it, I said, "OK, honey. Where's the rest of it?" And she said that was it. Well, it is customary in my culture to have a huge meal in the middle of the day – with the beans, the rice, a meat. So, needless to say, I was very surprised.

Hilary: This is Hilary García in Tepoztlán, Mexico. Back to you, Chris.

Chris: Thanks, Hilary, for helping us cross cultures. Next time I'm in Mexico, I'll remember to bring a big appetite when I'm invited to lunch. And we hope we've given you something to remember the next time you go abroad. Until next time, this is Chris Brooks for *Travel World,* bidding you "Bon voyage."

6 Heartbreak Hotel

A couple's hope for a relaxing weekend at a quaint hotel is dashed.

Walt: Eddie, I've got to run a few errands. Can you, uh, watch things for me till I get back?

Eddie: Well, sure, Walt. No problem.

• • •

Kim: Oh, what a quaint little hotel! You know, I'd much rather stay in a place like this than one of those big, fancy hotels. How on earth did you find this?

Mike: Well, I thought you might like it. I found it on the Internet. And the price is quite reasonable for this area.

• • •

Mike: I just can't wait to spend a relaxing weekend away from the office. No stress for two whole days.

Kim: Yeah, it's going to be great.

Mike: Hello. Anybody back there? It doesn't seem to be a very well-staffed hotel.

Eddie: I'm sorry. May I help you?

Mike: Yes. We have reservations.

Eddie: Name, please?

Mike: Johnson . . . Mike and Kim Johnson. For two nights.

Eddie: Uh-huh. . . . Yes, Mr. Johnson. You're in our VIP suite. How will you be paying for the room? Cash?

Mike: Uh, no. Credit card.

Eddie: Uh-huh. Mr. Johnson, would you fill this out, please? And sign here.

Mike: Sure. . . . There you go.

Eddie: Mm-hmm. Do you need any help with your luggage?

Mike: Uh, yes, that would be nice. . . .

Eddie: Follow me, please.

• • •

Eddie: OK. The remote control for the television is over there on the table. If your clothes are wrinkled from packing, you'll find an iron and an ironing board in the closet. The bedroom is through here. . . . Here is the temperature control. Push this button for air-conditioning, this button to turn on the heat; then adjust the temperature with this dial. There's a sink right here and another in the bathroom around the corner. Oh! . . . There's a hair dryer in case you need to dry your hair. . . . If there's anything else we can do for you, just call. The telephone's right over there.

Mike: OK, then. Well, I guess we're fine. Thanks. . . . Oh, I'm sorry. Of course. . . . Thanks.

Kim: He's a little strange, isn't he?

Mike: Very. I'm on vacation, and I'm already stressed out.

Kim: Oh, honey, he's gone now. Just let's relax. . . . Say, does it feel cold to you in here? I'm freezing, even with my jacket on.

Mike: Yeah. Look, the window's open. . . . It's stuck.

Kim: I'll turn on the heat. That should warm things up. . . . Hey, this thing's broken.

Mike: What happened?

Kim: I just touched it, and it came off in my hand.

Mike: I'm going to call the front desk. . . . I need to report a problem. We have a window that needs to be fixed, and the heat needs to be checked, too. Can you send someone up right away? . . . Thanks. . . . That was fast.

Kim: You again?

Eddie: OK, folks. What exactly is the problem?

Kim: Well, it's freezing cold in here.

Mike: That window needs to be fixed. It's stuck.

Eddie: Oh.

• • •

Kim: You know, it's still cold in here.

Eddie: Why don't you turn up the heat?

Mike: The heat doesn't work.

Eddie: What's wrong with it?

Kim: I pushed the button for heat, but when I tried to adjust the temperature, the knob came off in my hand.

Eddie: Hmm, I see. Well, to be honest with you, this may take some time to repair. Why don't you two just relax?

•   •   •

Eddie: There! Now it will be nice and warm. . . . Just let me know if you need anything else.

Kim: Thanks.

•   •   •

Kim: Well, it *is* getting warmer.

Mike: Yeah, but look around. The paint's cracked and peeling. The furniture's scratched. The curtains are torn. The carpet's worn and dirty. In fact, this place is a dump.

Kim: Well, it's kind of a quaint dump.

Mike: It's depressing.

Kim: I've got an idea: I'll make us a nice hot cup of tea.

Mike: That sounds good. . . . It's getting really warm in here. I think I'll turn the heat down a bit. . . . Kim? We have a little problem.

Kim: What?

Mike: The guy didn't fix the control. He just turned the temperature up. Now it's stuck on high. I can't turn the heat off.

Kim: Well, open the window again.

•   •   •

Mike: OK. I can't open it.

Kim: Uh, Mike, I'm afraid we have another problem.

Mike: What?

Kim: There's no water.

Mike: What next? This place is unbelievable. I'm going to call the front desk – again. . . . Great! Now there's no dial tone. That does it! Come on. We are leaving!

•   •   •

Mike: We are leaving!

Eddie: Is there something the matter?

Mike: Everything's the matter! First of all, the temperature control is still broken.

Kim: The room was freezing. Now it's too hot, and we can't control the heat.

Mike: The window is stuck – again. Now we can't open it.

Kim: There's no water, and even the telephone doesn't work.

Mike: In fact, nothing works! Everything is in need of repair. I want to see the manager.

Eddie: Of course, sir. Just a minute.

Mike: Can you believe this place? What else can go wrong?

Eddie: What exactly is the problem, folks?

Kim: You're the manager, too?

Eddie: That's what it says.

Mike: That does it! I want the charge taken off my card. We are not staying.

Eddie: Thanks for choosing the Heartbreak Hotel.

•   •   •

Walt: Hi, Eddie. Thanks for watching the place while I ran my errands.

Eddie: Happy to do it, Walt.

Walt: Anything happen while I was gone?

Eddie: Nothing I couldn't handle.

7 Saving Florida's manatees

Experts discuss conservation efforts to save Florida's manatees.

Narrator: It's a warm, sunny day in Florida. You decide to celebrate the beautiful weather by going out on your boat. While enjoying the sun and sea, you hear an unfamiliar sound. Looking out into the water to investigate, you spot a huge gray animal. Should you panic? Call for help? Of course not. Consider yourself lucky. You've just seen a manatee.... The West Indian manatee is a large aquatic mammal that looks like a blimp. Manatees, found in Florida as well as in parts of Central and South America and West Africa, evolved more than sixty million years ago. Their closest living relative today is the elephant.... The average adult male manatee weighs about a thousand pounds and can eat up to ten percent of its body weight in aquatic plants each day. Harmless and generally friendly to people, manatees have no natural predators. And with a normal life span of sixty years or more, you might think you would find a great many manatees in Florida's warm coastal waters. Unfortunately not. During the last survey, only twenty-six hundred were counted in the United States. These animals are being threatened by a variety of factors.... Their natural habitat has been reduced as a result of constantly expanding development, and what's left may be contaminated by pollution. Each year a large number of manatees are killed or seriously injured by fast-moving watercraft. Because manatees are slow and often swim near the surface, the propeller blades of speeding boats have too often been a cause of serious injury or death. Recognizing the threats to these creatures, both the United States government and the state of Florida have declared the manatee an endangered species, and today many efforts are being made to protect them and to increase their population.... One such effort is the Crystal River National Wildlife Refuge. Within this forty-six-acre site are several islands and bays devoted to providing and preserving habitat ideal for manatees.

Eileen Nuñez,
Park Ranger: There are several natural warm-water springs within King's Bay, which is where the refuge is located. And those warm-water springs provide the manatee a winter habitat in this area.

Narrator: Manatees, like people, will die of hypothermia if left in cold water for too long a period of time. They depend on these warm-water sources for their survival.

Eileen Nuñez: One way to recognize manatees in the area is by their telltale footprint on the surface of the water. They make a smooth, circular shape with their tail as they're swimming along. So when you see a smooth circle on the surface of the water, that usually means that there's a manatee nearby. Another sign to look for is the manatee's snout as they come to the surface to breathe.... They must breathe when they're active during the day every two to four minutes. And when they're sleeping and resting, manatees will generally come up and take a breath every fifteen to twenty minutes.

Narrator: In addition to preserving habitat, another way to help protect manatees and other endangered species is to educate the public.... Here at Homosassa Springs Wildlife Park, visitors can see Florida's wildlife up close in its natural environment. They can also learn why animals such as manatees are being threatened.

Betsy Dearth,
Park Ranger: Now, out in the wild, a lot of manatees get hit by boats and barges. We have one in here named Amanda – big scars on her back from being hit by a boat. They also get caught in crab traplines and fishing lines.

Narrator: During the summer months, many manatees leave the warm springs and move north along both coasts – sometimes ranging as far as Alabama in the Gulf of Mexico, and North Carolina and Virginia on the Atlantic coast. These migrations are being followed closely by researchers at the Florida Marine Research Institute.

FMRI

Researcher: Sometime here in February . . . uh . . . manatees return . . .

Narrator: Information they gather will help policy makers develop better strategies for protecting the manatee in the future. For more than thirty years, Dr. Buddy Powell has been studying manatees in Florida and in other countries such as Belize. He says research there helps them understand more about Florida's manatees.

Buddy Powell,

Ph.D., FMRI: It's been very, very interesting working there because we feel like we're actually getting a really good idea of what manatees would do in the absence of a lot of human activity. And again, that can relate back to how we think about manatee conservation in Florida.

Narrator: Another important part of the manatee conservation effort is to rescue and rehabilitate injured animals, then return them to their natural habitat. Here at SeaWorld® in Orlando, teams work to nurse manatees back to good health.

Randy Runnells,

SeaWorld®: We are the largest rehabilitator of manatees. Uh, we quite often get as many as twenty animals a year that . . . we . . . go through our rehab program.

Narrator: The efforts of the veterinarians and biologists at SeaWorld® have paid off. Today three manatees, now back in good health, are being returned to the wild. . . .

Recently, the manatee population has been gradually increasing as a result of the efforts of many people. So why is it important to continue to spend so much time and money on this seemingly insignificant creature? Perhaps it has to do with our own well-being.

Man: I think they're kind of like a sign of how the environment's doing. And if manatees can survive alongside us, I think our environment's going to be doing well.

Woman 1: We're not only providing and protecting habitat for a wildlife species, but we're also preserving a healthy habitat for ourselves.

Woman 2: We're the ones that have to do something about it; otherwise, our children and their children might not see manatees.

•   •   •

Narrator: To find out more about the manatee and what you can do to help save this gentle giant, visit the Save the Manatee Club on the World Wide Web at www.savethemanatee.org.

8 Salsa!

People all over the world are learning how to dance salsa.

Billy Kimmel,
Narrator: You've probably been taking classes for as long as you can remember. But today learning doesn't end when you earn a diploma. Learning has become a lifelong pursuit – for career advancement and just for fun. What interests *you*? Would you prefer to brush up on your math skills or improve your chess game? Would you rather learn English or take a class in the latest software program? There certainly are a lot of choices, but not all learning takes place in traditional classrooms or from books.

• • •

Billy Kimmel: From tap to tango, and samba to swing, learning to dance is one of today's hottest trends. And salsa dancing is the hottest of them all. Its popularity has quickly spread all over the world. . . . Hi. I'm Billy Kimmel. During the next few minutes, we're going to visit some dance classes and clubs and get some advice on how to dance salsa style.

Rico's Dance Studio – Tokyo, Japan

Billy Kimmel: How's your dance class going?

Woman 1: It's fun!

Man 1: It's great!

Billy Kimmel: Why did you decide to take a salsa class?

Woman 1: Because I was interested in dance.

Man 1: Because a lot of our friends come here.

Billy Kimmel: What's the best way to improve your dancing?

Woman 1: By going out to nightclubs.

Man 1: By practicing hard.

• • •

Billy Kimmel: You seem to be doing really well. How did you learn to dance like that?

Man 2: By coming to class every weekend.

Billy Kimmel: Now, why did you decide to take salsa lessons?

Man 2: Because . . . uh . . . my buddy from high school just opened up . . . uh . . . like a salsa class, and, uh, he just invited me, so I joined it.

Shin's Dance Studio – Seoul, Korea

Billy Kimmel: How did you learn to dance salsa?

Woman 2: Uh, I took some lessons.

Billy Kimmel: What's a good way to improve your dancing?

Woman 2: Uh, by practicing with a guy. But you have to find the . . . a good partner.

Woman 3: By moving to the music!

Man 3 and Woman 4: By just dancing!

Quest Dance Club – United States

Billy Kimmel: It's salsa night at the Quest Dance Club. People are here for some dance lessons before the band arrives. Rebecca Trost teaches salsa here at the Quest. . . . Rebecca, why do you think salsa is so popular these days?

Rebecca Trost: I think people like the . . . uh . . . hypnotic rhythms of salsa. I think it appeals to a wide variety of people. I think . . . uh . . . they like to have something easy to do and, uh, enjoy the music as well.

Billy Kimmel: What do you recommend for people who want to learn salsa?

Rebecca Trost: I would recommend taking private lessons and/or group classes and then practicing.

Billy Kimmel: And what's a good way to improve your salsa dancing?

Rebecca Trost: Going out to the nightclubs, practicing out in the nightclubs, getting together with friends at parties or even in your own home.

• • •

Billy Kimmel: How long have you been coming here?

Man 4: I've been coming here for about six years to Quest every Monday night . . . uh . . . because I love to dance salsa.

Billy Kimmel: And what is it about salsa dancing that you like?

Man 4: I think salsa, I mean, it's got . . . it's got a good driving beat, it's got a lot of passion to it, and I think that it's a fun type of partner dance.

Billy Kimmel: And do you have any advice for people who are thinking about learning salsa dancing?

Man 4: I think a lot of people who don't know they . . . uh . . . if they can really dance until they get out and try. I think dancing starts by taking the initiative. Take a class.

• • •

Billy Kimmel: You're looking good out there. What brings you to the Quest on salsa night?

Man 5: Well, I come here to dance . . . um . . . because I like salsa. I'm from Puerto Rico, and I grew up . . . uh . . . going to the pubs and festivals – salsa festivals.

Billy Kimmel: Why do you think salsa is so popular?

Man 5: Because it is basically a mix of so many trends and cultures into one type of music, I think it is appealing to people. And also because it's . . . uh . . . really upbeat and people like that . . . uh . . . when they go dancing.

• • •

Billy Kimmel: You seem to be enjoying yourself. Do you come here often?

Woman 5: Yes. I come here just about every week. I come here to dance.

Billy Kimmel: Why do you think salsa is so popular?

Woman 5: You don't learn a set of steps. You just listen to the music and interpret the music.

Billy Kimmel: What's the best way to learn salsa dancing? Any recommendations?

Woman 5: It depends on how you learn. Some people learn best by going to a class. I learn best by watching and listening to the music and then getting brave and trying it a little.

Billy Kimmel: Do you prefer taking lessons in a studio or going out to a club?

Woman 5: I prefer coming to a club and dancing here. There's a different energy; it's more social. But there's nothing wrong with taking lessons. I recommend it.

• • •

Billy Kimmel: You're a great dancer. How did you get started? Did you take lessons?

Man 6: When I first started dancing, there weren't . . . there weren't really any schools around to learn from, so what I did was . . . um . . . I listened to salsa in the car – just about everywhere – to get familiar with the music and the rhythm. And then . . . um . . . on Sunday mornings, I'd wake up, put on the fastest salsa that I could, and just do the steps.

Billy Kimmel: Do you have any advice for people who want to learn salsa dancing?

Man 6: Learn by doing. Practice, practice . . . uh . . . yeah, exactly. Just practice.

Billy Kimmel: That's a good idea. Maybe I should try that. How hard can it be?

• • •

Billy Kimmel: OK, how do I get started?

Woman 6: Well, you can start by learning your basic rhythms and steps. Follow me. Quick, quick, slow. Quick, quick, slow. Quick, quick, slow.

Billy Kimmel: Quick, quick, slow. . . .

• • •

Billy Kimmel: OK, I think I've got it.

Woman 6: I think you do! You're a natural.

Billy Kimmel: Hey, this is a lot of fun. You should try it. This is Billy Kimmel, actually salsa dancing, from the Quest Dance Club.

9 Stress relief

A woman seeks advice from a co-worker on how to relieve stress.

Margie: Ah! This has got to stop.

John: What is it, Margie? You look so stressed out.

Margie: John, it's this job. I'm under pressure all the time. My muscles are tense. My stomach is upset. I just can't seem to relax. What can I do?

John: Yeah, stress. It's a killer. Well, one thing you could do is exercise. It really helps me when I'm stressed out, and it's a great way to blow off steam.

Margie: Well, actually, I've tried that. First I took up Rollerblading®, . . . but that didn't work. Then I . . . I tried dancing lessons, . . . but I couldn't find a good dance partner.

John: Well, what about swimming? There's a health club with a swimming pool just down the street. It's really good exercise, and being in the water is so relaxing.

Margie: That's not a bad idea, . . . except I can't swim.

      •   •   •

John: Well, have you thought about taking a yoga class? I hear that yoga's very relaxing.

      •   •   •

Margie: Oh, I don't know. . . . I . . . I don't think yoga's the right thing for me.

John: Well, there's hypnotherapy.

Margie: You know what? You're not going to believe this, but I've tried that, too. . . . OK, it's like this. Every time I hear the word *ocean,* I'm supposed to relax. And it works. In fact, it works too well. Once when I was in an important business meeting, someone started talking about "ocean" ecology. People said the word *ocean* so many times that I fell asleep.

John: Oh, you know, I think I remember that. I thought you were sick or something. It must have been embarrassing.

Margie: You can say that again! Now everybody in the office knows about it. People pass my office and make snoring sounds.

John: Oh, I'm sorry. Hey, I have an idea. Maybe you could try aromatherapy.

Margie: What's that?

John: Well, first they put you in a softly lit room, and then they open different jars and let you smell them.

      •   •   •

Margie: Oh, well, I . . . I don't know. I'm allergic to most perfumes. You know what, John? I don't think any of those things are going to be right for me.

John: Or it might be a good idea to take some time off. Go on a little trip – maybe a little beach vacation by the ocean.

Margie: Hmm. [*yawns*] That's a good idea. I'm feeling better already. Thanks, John. You've been a great help.

John: Anytime. Hey, enjoy your trip to the ocean.

Margie: [*yawns*] Thanks. [*yawns*]

10 Fort Steele Heritage Town

Visitors to Fort Steele in Canada get transported back in time.

Narrator: You may think it's the twenty-first century, but in Fort Steele Heritage Town, it's still the 1890s. Fort Steele is a living museum. Here, visitors can transport themselves back in time to see how people in a Canadian frontier town lived.

Noel Ratch,
Program Manager: We really try to keep an atmosphere of what it was like in the 1890s here on the site. Uh, we want to give people a full experience of what it was like to live back then.

Narrator: Fort Steele is located in Canada's westernmost province of British Columbia, in the heart of the Rocky Mountains and just north of the U.S.-Canadian border. So, what was it like in Canada during the nineteenth century? The late 1800s were a period of westward expansion and development in Canada. Some people were moving west, seeking their fortunes in the gold fields. Others came to claim land for farms and ranches. The shopkeepers and tradesmen came soon after, offering goods and services to the new settlers. New frontier towns were born. Fort Steele was a typical town of that period. It began as a ferry crossing over the Kootenay River, providing a way for miners to reach the gold fields. Then, in 1898, the Canadian Pacific Railway located their new rail line through the neighboring town of Cranbrook. Within a few years, the population of Fort Steele was reduced to a couple of hundred. For more than fifty years, the town was deserted. Then some local citizens decided they wanted to restore this fascinating piece of local history.

Martin Ross,
General Manager: Fort Steele Heritage Town was started in 1961, largely through the efforts of interested community members who wanted to preserve this . . . uh . . . significant historic site. Now we have over sixty . . . uh . . . restored historic buildings, including a theater, restaurant, bakery, and lots of other attractions.

Narrator: One of those attractions is the Royal Canadian Mounted Police Post. The Royal Canadian Mounted Police were Canada's answer to keeping law and order in frontier settlements.

Jim Robinson,
Mountie
Interpreter: They came as peacemakers. There was never a shot fired. There was never anything like that done here. They solved all of their problems through words rather than violence.

• • •

Jim Robinson: (*to group of children*) Do you understand this, Constables?

Children: Yes, sir, Sergeant Major Sauer, sir!

Narrator: Today, those up to the challenge can experience what life was like for the mounties, the ordinary enlisted men (called constables), and the officers like Superintendent Sam Steele, for whom the town was eventually named. Through other displays and interpreters, visitors can learn what it was like to live without electricity, running water, and many of the twenty-first-century comforts we take for granted.

Stephanie Pfeiffer,
Lambi House
Interpreter: In the 1890s, families didn't have any running hot or cold water. Instead, they would have to use a pump to get their water. . . . And for any hot water they wanted, they would have to heat it on the stove.

Narrator: At Fort Steele, visitors can also see how tradesmen performed their work and learn about the vital roles they played in the frontier community.

Paul Reimer,
Blacksmith: The blacksmith was a very important person in any . . . uh . . . pioneer community. They kept the horses . . . um . . . with shoes on their feet, which kept them from damaging their hooves. They also made wagons . . . and wheels . . . and all kinds of tools that a farmer

(continued)

would have used, would have been fixed or repaired or built by a blacksmith.

Narrator: Those who wonder what school was like in the 1890s can attend Miss Bailey's class at Fort Steele School.

**Wynne Royer
as Teacher,
"Miss Bailey":** Good afternoon, boys and girls.

Students: Good afternoon, Miss Bailey.

Wynne Royer: Excellent. It is like music to my ears. Boys and girls, . . .

Narrator: Wynne Royer plays the role of Miss Bailey, the teacher who taught at Fort Steele School in the 1890s.

Wynne Royer: This would be a typical classroom. This is actually . . . uh . . . quite a nice school, being as it has two classrooms. There's a second one right next door. Within these two classrooms, she would have taught grades one through eight. . . . (*to a student*) Good for you, dear. You remembered that you are meant to raise your hand.

Narrator: As you walk through the streets, you may encounter other characters from Fort Steele's past who will make life in the 1890s come alive.

Mule Owner: I'm a short-distance hauler. Well, actually, Angelica here does the hauling, and I just lead her around.

Narrator: If you're hungry, stop for lunch at the International Hotel or try some coffee and pastries at Fort Steele's bakery. And what does the future hold for this historic town?

Martin Ross: Canadians are becoming more and more interested in history, so over the next few years, we predict that, uh, more and more visitors will be coming to Fort Steele. So we like to add new attractions each year. Our old-time trades like our blacksmith, tinsmith, and harness maker have been very popular, so I think that we'll be adding maybe a boot maker or hatmaker in the future.

Store Clerk: OK. There you go.

Customer: Thank you.

Narrator: So if you need a break from the hectic pace of the twenty-first century, or if you are just curious about what life was like in a nineteenth-century Canadian frontier town, come visit Fort Steele Heritage Town – alive and booming once again.

11 If only ...

Five college friends get together to talk about their past, present, and future.

Deanna: I think they're coming.

. . .

Pamela: Yeah, me, too! Just like when we were in college. . . . Now, how about some of my mother's special chocolate cake for dessert?

Roberta: OK.

. . .

Amelia, Deanna,
Laura: Surprise! Happy birthday!

Roberta: Oh, you guys! I really thought you had forgotten.

Pamela: Who, me? Forget?

Roberta: You didn't say anything the whole night. I had no idea.

. . .

Amelia: Hey, guys. Guys! Before we open presents and have birthday cake, how about looking at a few pictures?

Deanna: Oh, no!

Amelia: OK. Here goes.

Roberta: Oh, look at Deanna: always the serious one.

Amelia: Even then, you were hard at work.

Deanna: I know. I should have been more carefree like the rest of you. I never learned to relax.

Laura: Oh, but you were so sensible. You always did well in school and graduated at the top of your class.

Roberta: Yeah. Now look at you. You are a successful lawyer.

Deanna: Yes, but I didn't think that having a good time in college was important. The moment I graduated, I realized I had missed a lot. I still don't know how to relax and have fun.

Pamela: Well, Deanna, if I had listened to you, I wouldn't be just a clerk at the office. I'd be the manager.

Deanna: What do you mean?

. . .

Deanna: Oh, Pamela, don't you think you should study for your exams?

Pamela: Yeah. Yeah, after this.

. . .

Deanna: Oh, yeah.

Pamela: But, hey! Now I'm taking classes at night, and I hope to earn my degree in business administration.

Roberta: But you have to study, Pamela.

Pamela: I know, I know.

Amelia: And look at me. I'm still waiting tables. I'm not the big actress I dreamed of becoming.

Roberta: Look. Remember this?

. . .

Deanna: You were fantastic that night.

Amelia: I was so naive. I thought that just being a good actress was the key to success. If I'd been more realistic, I would have majored in education. At least now, I could be teaching drama instead of waiting tables.

Laura: Don't worry, Amelia. You'll make it.

Roberta: Yeah, before you know it, you'll be a famous movie star, and we'll all have to line up to get your autograph.

Laura: May I have your autograph, please?

Amelia: Autograph, right. We'll be asking for *your* autograph soon.

Deanna: Yeah. The Internet genius.

Laura: I am a long way from being that famous, guys. I'm ambitious, yes, but not famous.

Roberta: All those long hours in front of the computer sure paid off.

. . .

Laura: Seven A.M.! My exam!

. . .

Deanna: You lost a lot of sleep, but if you hadn't been so dedicated, you'd never have become president of your own Internet company.

(continued)

Laura: I guess that's true.

Pamela: And what about you, Roberta? Have you finally decided what you want to do?

Amelia: You certainly have traveled a lot.

Roberta: Yes, I have. But it's time to settle down into a career. The moment I took my first trip, I knew what I wanted to be.

Deanna: What's that?

Roberta: A travel agent!

Pamela: That's perfect!

Roberta: I took a lot of business, but I should have majored in languages. Knowing different languages can really help when you're in the travel industry.

Amelia: We agree. That's why . . . we got you these.

Deanna: Go ahead, open it.

Roberta: Oh! Just what I needed! . . . This is so . . . – Thanks, you guys!

12 Need information? AskJeeves.com

The success of an Internet search engine company is discussed.

Narrator: We live in the Information Age, and with the amount of knowledge in the world doubling every ten to fifteen years, how do you keep up? Well, you can use the Internet. But when you log on, how do you find the information you want? One way is to "ask Jeeves." What is Ask Jeeves? It's an Internet site that answers requests for information. And Jeeves, a helpful butler, is your guide for finding answers on the Ask Jeeves Web site. Each day, users ask Jeeves all kinds of questions: Who won World Cup soccer in 1992? How do computers work? Where can I buy a DVD player online?

**Penny Finnie,
Vice President
of Ideas:** Most people, when they get on the Internet, don't really know where to go. And so they use search engines to find out what sites are out there in their areas of interest. Most search engines, you just go and you type in one word. So if you wanted to buy a car, you would type in *cars*. But what comes back is a long, long, long, long list of all of the car sites out there. With Jeeves, it's different. Um, if you want to buy a car online, you go and you say, "Where can I buy a car online?" And Jeeves takes you to the sites that answer that question.

**Marjorie Stout,
Content Editor:** Ask Jeeves is different because it's really a question-and-answer service. You come to Jeeves and you ask a question. The answers we . . . we return to our users are in the form of another question. And so you pick the question that Jeeves gives you that's most similar to the one that you asked, and behind that question is your answer.

Narrator: The popularity of the site has grown rapidly. Just a few years ago, Ask Jeeves was answering about five hundred questions a month. Now that number has risen to more than 11 million a month, and it's still growing. So, how did this Internet company become so successful?

In order for any business to succeed, it has to begin with a good concept. Ask Jeeves was born in Berkeley, California, in 1995. It was the brainchild of computer scientist David Warthen and venture capitalist Garrett Gruener. Their idea was to make Internet use a more human experience. To do this, they wanted a character on their Web site that users could interact with.

Penny Finnie: We wanted to make somebody that was approachable, that was trustworthy, that . . . uh . . . people would feel comfortable asking questions of. We . . . We thought about a librarian. We thought about a wizard. We thought about a professor. But, um, we realized that the butler sort of might be broader and could do more things for you.

Narrator: The result of their efforts was the helpful character of Jeeves the Butler. Jeeves is the namesake of another character made famous in a series of books written by P. G. Wodehouse beginning in the 1920s. For a Web site like Ask Jeeves to be successful, it also has to have good marketing. The character of Jeeves has inspired some unique marketing campaigns. John Perry is senior marketing writer at Ask Jeeves.

**John Perry, Senior
Marketing Writer:** We have what we call the "Butler Blast." Um, that's when we go to a city and hire a group of actors and dress them like Jeeves and send them spontaneously into . . . um . . . a place like Wall Street or Santa Monica along the beach or at the opening of a mall. And we have this group of . . . um . . . interesting, intriguing gentlemen helping people with their shopping, giving them directions, handing out . . . um . . . free things. Very often the "Butler Blast" will attract the attention . . . um . . . of the local news, so we get TV coverage, we'll get noticed in newspapers and magazines.

•　•　•

(continued)

We've sent Jeeves to participate in the Macy's Thanksgiving Day Parade. We were very excited to have him become one of the giant balloons that floats down Broadway. The parade is the largest in America. Millions and millions of people watch it, not just in the U.S., but around the world.

• • •

We arranged with several of the major fruit companies to create fruit labels. Millions of pieces of fruit were sold with stickers on them that asked questions related to the fruits themselves. And then they included Jeeves's face and the Web address . . . um . . . where people could go and get the answer. We were able to track those . . . questions and those Web addresses on the site, and we found it was immensely popular.

Narrator: Clever marketing campaigns will bring people to the site, but to get them to come back again and again, you need to provide the information they're looking for. That's where the Ask Jeeves content editors come in.

Marjorie Stout: The most important issue for us as editors is to stay on top of trends and to make sure that we're really delivering what our users want.

Monte Luke,
Content Editor: First of all, first and foremost is researching the Web for the best answer – meaning the best Web site . . . um . . . to answer whatever the particular question is.

Narrator: Despite the fact that users aren't charged for coming to the site, Ask Jeeves has been financially successful. Let's talk with Steve Roop, director of sales.

Steve Roop,
Director of Sales: One of the things that's important to the success of any business is that business's ability to generate revenue. And Ask Jeeves makes . . . uh . . . revenue, or makes its money, in three different ways.

The first way is on the Ask Jeeves or Ask.com Web site. And the Web site basically charges advertisers money to advertise their products and services right on the Ask.com Web site. So that's way number one.

Number two: Companies pay for placement on the Ask Jeeves site. So if I am a health-services company and I want my . . . content to show up on Ask Jeeves, I can pay Ask Jeeves . . . uh . . . to show that content on the Web site.

A very good example of "pay for placement" is our relationship with Health Central. Health Central provides all sorts of health content to users. So if someone asks the question, "How do I know if my baby has an earache?" then it's going to take them to Health Central's content. So that's way number two.

And way number three is Ask Jeeves licenses its technology and implements its technology on major corporate Web sites, like Nike® – Nike® the footwear maker. So if you go to the Nike® Web site and say, "I want high-performance basketball shoes for under $85," Ask Jeeves technology will actually go into their product catalog and find just the basketball shoes that match your criteria.

So the three ways in which we make our money is: number one, through advertising revenue; two, through paid placement; and three, by licensing our technology to large corporations.

Narrator: A good concept, a unique search engine, clever marketing ideas, revenue sources to support the organization. It seems Ask Jeeves has all the right answers to running a successful business. Jeeves may also have the answers you're looking for.

13 Car trouble

A groom and his best man get delayed on the way to the wedding.

Sam: We shouldn't have spent so much time at that gift shop.

Bill: Ah, I did the right thing. The top of the wedding cake is everything! Besides, this shortcut will get us there with time to spare.

Sam: I still think we should have stayed on Highway 41. Did you remember the ring? Bill, you did not forget it?

Bill: Relax. It's right here. What time does the ceremony begin?

Sam: Three o'clock.

Bill: And what time is it now?

Sam: It's 1:30.

Bill: Good! We have plenty of time.

Sam: Yeah, but we have to be there an hour early for pictures. That only gives us half an hour.

Bill: Trust me. We're almost there.

Sam: Except for that "Road Closed" sign ahead!

•   •   •

Emily: OK, Debbie. Twenty minutes to the start of the biggest event in my life. Sam and Bill must have left by now.

Debbie: Stop worrying, Emily. What could go wrong?

•   •   •

Bill: See? I knew that shortcut would work. Now we're right back on schedule.

Sam: Except for that warning light that just went on.

•   •   •

Sam: Oh, great! Now we're really going to be late.

Bill: Just relax, Sam. I know this car inside and out. I will have it fixed in a – [*coughs*]

•   •   •

Emily: Where are they? Do you think they might have gotten lost . . . or they may have missed a turn or something?

Debbie: There's no way you can get lost if you stay on Highway 41.

Emily: I hope not. The photographer will be here any minute.

•   •   •

Sam: Now we're never going to get there on time.

Bill: We will if you stop whining and go get some water from that farmhouse over there.

•   •   •

Emily: I wonder what could have happened!

Debbie: They might not have remembered about being here early for the pictures.

Emily: Oh, Sam wouldn't have forgotten. He's a very responsible person.

Debbie: They might have had car trouble or something. Bill's car is really an old clunker.

Emily: Debbie, you're my bridesmaid. You're supposed to be reassuring me.

Debbie: Sorry.

•   •   •

Sam: Anything?

Bill: You know? We might be out of gas.

Sam: My life is over.

Bill: Why don't you go get some gas from that farmer so we can get back on the road?

•   •   •

Emily: Where are they?

Debbie: They could have . . . um . . . gotten in an accident.

Emily: Debbie!

Debbie: I meant a little one.

Emily: [*cries*]

•   •   •

Bill: The good news is we're not out of gas. The bad news is the car still won't start.

Sam: The bad news is your life is over!

Bill: Oh, get a hold of yourself, Sam! I promised I would get you there on time, and I intend to keep my promise.

(continued)

Sam: How?

Bill: I haven't figured that out yet.

      •   •   •

Emily: Do you see any cars pulling up?

Debbie: No. Just an old hay wagon with a farmer and two guys in tuxedos.

Emily: What?

      •   •   •

Emily: Sam, what happened?

Sam: It's a long story.

Bill: Don't be so shy, Sam. He thought an old-fashioned country wedding deserved a real country arrival.

Emily: Oh! Well, hurry up. They're all waiting for us.

14 Behind the scenes in TV news

A look at how TV news is produced.

Narrator: Have you ever wondered how the news gets produced? There's a lot more involved than you might think. For people who are watching, it appears simple. But it's always a challenge to complete a news show. Here at KMSP–TV, we're going to see how the evening news, or newscast as it is commonly called, is produced, by talking to some of the people who make it happen. Let's start with the associate news director, Alan Beck. The associate news director, who is often an experienced journalist, is the person that's in charge of daily operations. He says he's also the person who has to exercise good news judgment.

Alan Beck,
Associate News
Director: I decide what stories we cover, what reporters are assigned to what stories, how much time and resource we will devote to a particular story. It's really more of a team effort than I think most people realize. We are consulting with each other all the time.

Narrator: After decisions are made on what news stories have to be covered, the focus is on the assignment editor, Keith Brown. He is the team member that decides where the photographers and reporters will go.

Keith Brown,
Assignment Editor: Uh, my job is to . . . uh . . . to gather all the information story ideas from the public, from our reporters, from wire services. Then I will decide what crews to assign to it – what reporters, what photographers.

Narrator: The reporter is the person that gets the information and writes the script for the story. The photographer is the one who shoots the pictures and gets the sound to go along with the story. Rod Wermager is a news photographer here at Channel 9.

Rod Wermager,
Photographer: It's . . . It's kind of a collaboration between me and . . . and the reporter in terms of the video that needs to be shot, how it needs to be shot.

Narrator: Vince Irby is the other half of the team.
Vince Irby,
Reporter: The reporter is the person who comes in at the beginning of the day, discusses possible story ideas with an assignment editor, with a producer, . . . uh . . . and then basically gets on the phone and he starts making calls to set up that story, or goes right out to the scene.

Rod Wermager: Once we get everything documented on tape, we bring it back here to the station . . . uh . . . where the reporter will then grab the tapes, look at the pictures I've got, look at his sound bites, pick out sound bites he wants to use in his news story. He gets the script done. Uh, he cuts the audio track.

Narrator: The photographer, who is also a video editor, then takes the soundtrack and the videotape and edits them into a finished news story.

Vince Irby: Rod puts it together. And it's . . . it's really magical how it all comes together.

Narrator: So what happens after the stories for the nightly news show are edited together? Let's meet the news show's producer, Carrie Hoerrmann.

Carrie Hoerrmann,
Producer: The producer is the person who is sort of the manager of the newscast – the boss of the newscast. I decide what stories go into the newscast, what order, how much time to give each story. With the use of the computer, I wipe out the previous day's rundown and start over – clean slate.

Narrator: The producer is like a newspaper editor. She selects which stories to include in the newscast and in what order. She proofreads and edits the stories, and she decides how they will be presented: by the anchor on camera or with graphics.

Carrie Hoerrmann: About an hour before the newscast, we want ninety percent of the newscast written. Then we print it.

(continued)

Narrator: During the newscast, the producer sits in the control room to make sure the script is being followed. But in the control room, the director is in charge.

Leo Hofmeister, Director: The director is a person who gets the script from a producer and coordinates all the efforts of the technical staff to get a newscast on the air.

Narrator: The staff in the control room includes an assistant director, an audio person, a technical person, an assistant to the technical person, and a graphic artist. The director is also responsible for telling the news anchors which camera to look at and for telling the camera operators what angles and shots he wants them to get.

Leo Hofmeister: One of the most exciting things about my job in TV news is that it's live. There is absolutely no opportunity to have retakes, so if I make a mistake here, it's something that you're going to see at home.

Narrator: The anchors are the people viewers see delivering the news. At this station, there are two: a man and a woman. Robyne Robinson is one of the anchors.

Robyne Robinson, Anchor: Every anchor's job is different. But what we usually do every day is we try to read as much as we can, listen to as much radio as we can . . . uh . . . watch as much news on the other stations and on the network news as possible. We take that information, and we write scripts all day long with the help of writers and producers and the reporters and photographers.

Narrator: After the preparation, Robyne and her co-anchor are the ones who deliver the news to the public.

Jeff Passolt, Anchor: It wouldn't be the Minnesota State Fair without Princess Kay of the Milky Way.

Robyne Robinson: And tonight the decision has been made. Who is going to reign over the fair as Princess Kay? Well, Vince Irby is live at the fairgrounds with the contest and more on the winner.

Vince Irby: Brigette Hollerman just took the stage. She just took the crown. And we're going to do a pan-over and see if we can see her. She is being embraced and hugged by her friends. She just took that on live TV. You saw it here about two minutes ago. She's twenty years old. She's from Farwell, Minnesota –

Robyne Robinson: Ninety-nine percent of the stories are pre-scripted, but we like to add a little of our own personality to it. So we may ad-lib just a little bit. And there's always the cross talk between anchors that's not scripted. Some nights it's perfect, wonderful, flawless, no mistakes. Some nights it's a circus, and things go wrong: and the TelePrompTer® doesn't work, and you go from one camera to the next and it's the wrong camera and you're looking the wrong way, or you just stumble all over yourself. But that's what makes it fun. You know, every night is different. It's live.

Narrator: It's eleven o'clock. The newscast is over, and it's time to go home. Tomorrow the members of the news team will return once more to start the process all over again. The associate director will decide what stories to follow. The assignment editor will gather the story ideas and assign reporters and photographers to cover them. The photographers and reporters will gather the pictures, sound, and information they need to tell a news story. The producer will create a script for the newscast by deciding which stories will be included, how they'll be presented, and in what order. Following the producer's script, the director will tell the technical staff what to do to get the newscast on the air. Finally, the anchors will deliver the news. And that's how it works every day behind the scenes in TV news.

Environment or entertainment? A town debates.

The building of an amphitheater stirs controversy among citizens.

Adam Whisner,
Narrator: It's a quiet, serene place now. But just a few years ago, this was a noisy, dirty garbage dump. Now developers are proposing to build an outdoor amphitheater to host live entertainment shows, such as operas, symphonies, rock concerts, and more, during the warm months of the year. But this project has stirred up quite a bit of controversy in the city of Burnsville, where the amphitheater would be built, and in neighboring communities.

Hi. I'm Adam Whisner, and I'm standing on the site of the controversial project, the Burnsville Amphitheater. Burnsville is a suburb of Minneapolis, Minnesota, and it's located on the bank of an important river that flows through the area. According to its supporters, the amphitheater is an opportunity to turn a little-used piece of land into an attractive outdoor entertainment center. It would seat almost 20,000 people and provide a new source of revenue for the city. On top of that, the city would not have to finance an environmental cleanup of the former dump site. That would be paid for by the developers. It seems like a good idea, doesn't it? So what's the controversy?

Well, right next to the project site is a national wildlife refuge, and just across the river are the homes of many people who are afraid of the noise, traffic congestion, and disruption they believe the project would bring. They think the city shouldn't be allowed to build it. We're going to talk to people on both sides of this issue and see how they feel about it – and why.

The Minnesota Valley National Wildlife Refuge is a sanctuary for many species. Joe Artmann, a Burnsville resident and wildlife biologist, is concerned about what will happen to these animals and birds if the amphitheater is built.

Joe Artmann,
Wildlife biologist: This amphitheater proposal is going to have a dramatic impact on the animals and the birds that utilize the area.

The sporadic loud noises, the impact of nearly 20,000 people, and thousands of vehicles will scare wildlife out of the area. It will cause increased mortality and may disrupt the reproductive behavior of some species. I'd prefer to see the area incorporated either into the national wildlife refuge system or be left as a natural area.

Adam Whisner: Greg Konat, Burnsville's city manager, doesn't think that the refuge will be in danger, since the noise already produced by nearby Interstate Highway 35W has not affected the wildlife at all.

Greg Konat,
City Manager
of Burnsville: The impact on the wildlife refuge was analyzed, and interestingly enough, the sound level being generated by Interstate 35W . . . uh . . . which goes right along the wildlife refuge, was actually louder than what we anticipate the amphitheater would be. There isn't any indication . . . uh . . . that it's going to have a negative impact on the wildlife . . . uh . . . in the area.

Adam Whisner: However, in Artmann's opinion, the continuous noise of automobile traffic and the sporadic loud noises of occasional concerts shouldn't be compared.

Joe Artmann: Studies have shown that most species of wildlife will adapt to continuous regular noise levels such as traffic noise. But occasional loud and unfamiliar noises have been shown to have significant negative impacts.

Adam Whisner: Residents in Bloomington, a community just across the river from the proposed project, are also opposed to the potential noise. Many of them feel that something has got to be done to stop it. Brian Carlson is one homeowner who thinks the amphitheater project shouldn't be permitted to go forward.

(continued)

Brian Carlson,
Bloomington
homeowner: As far as we personally are concerned at our home, we're very concerned about the noise. We know that the way it's being proposed and designed, it will be troublesome and create a noise problem for our neighbors and . . . and ourselves.

Adam Whisner: Burnsville's city manager doesn't think noise will be a problem.

Greg Konat: There is a significant amount of controls placed on the operator of the amphitheater. There will be . . . uh . . . monitoring devices both in Burnsville and in Bloomington that will . . . um . . . be monitoring the sound levels while the concerts are going on.

Adam Whisner: Residents are also concerned about the increased amount of traffic the amphitheater will bring.

Man 1: I think that something must be done to stop this project. . . . In my opinion, it's going to create enormous problems with traffic. I live here in Burnsville, and I don't want any more car and truck traffic than we already have.

Adam Whisner: Burnsville's city manager says the project will actually help improve the highway system.

Greg Konat: Roadways will be built to help traffic flow both to and from the site in a more efficient way. All of those roadways would then be used year-round . . . uh . . . by the people in Burnsville and the people that come to our area.

Adam Whisner: Elizabeth Kautz, mayor of Burnsville, says that the amphitheater is a good use for the former garbage dump. It will actually bring environmental benefits to the city, and taxpayers will not have to finance a costly cleanup project.

Elizabeth Kautz,
Mayor of Burnsville: The amphitheater project is a project that will allow us to reclaim the riverfront and to begin the cleanup of the riverfront so that our citizens can access the river.

Adam Whisner: Burnsville's city manager agrees.

Greg Konat: The amphitheater . . . uh . . . would allow us to close the landfill in an environmentally sound way.

Adam Whisner: City officials also cite another benefit the amphitheater will bring: revenue, in the form of taxes.

Greg Konat: It'd provide economic development because the amphitheater itself will generate taxes that will be used to build infrastructure.

Adam Whisner: Ordinary citizens we talked to had mixed reactions to the project.

Woman 1: I think that location-wise, it's perfect. So if it means bringing in more revenue and obviously more culture to this area, then I'm all for it – definitely. And I would go.

Man 2: I think it'd be a nice idea. I've been to a couple of different amphitheaters in different parts of the country, and it's . . . it's nice being outside listening to the music and whatever is being played at the time – and the sun's going down, and it's . . . it's just very comfortable and relaxing.

Man 3: I think it will bring some good things to the economy. And, uh, that's always good!

Woman 2: I don't think it's a very good idea because I think that some of the music groups, like the rock and heavy-metal bands, will create a lot of noise. And another thing is the kind of behavior that type of music provokes. People tend to drink too much, and there's often drug use. And I just think they shouldn't be allowed to build it here.

Brian Carlson: In my opinion, it's a disaster. I don't think it should be built. Uh, it has enormous environmental problems associated with it. There's water-pollution problems associated with it. So I think basically it's a . . . it's a bad plan and a bad idea.

Adam Whisner: You've heard some of the facts and some of the opinions surrounding this issue: the benefits of reclaiming a former garbage dump; the city's redevelopment plans; potential problems with noise, traffic, and the environment and how they'll be dealt with. You've listened to both sides. Should the amphitheater be built or not? This is Adam Whisner, reporting from the city of Burnsville.

16 The ultimate challenge

Four women cross Antarctica without the help of dogs, machine, or men.

Narrator: What's the most challenging thing you've managed to accomplish? Training for and running a marathon? Completing your college degree? Maybe learning to program your own Web site? How about crossing Antarctica on skis, pulling a 110-kilo sled? That's what four women from the United States decided to do. The expedition was the idea of Ann Bancroft, a former teacher and winter-trekking enthusiast from St. Paul, Minnesota. Her dream was to cross Antarctica totally under her own power without dogs, machines, or men. Her partners for the expedition were Sue Giller, a computer programmer and outdoor enthusiast from Boulder, Colorado, who would be the navigator for the expedition; Anne Dal-Vera, also from Colorado, who had extensive winter-camping experience and was the team's strongest skier; and Sunniva Sorby from San Diego, California, also a winter-camping enthusiast with extensive wilderness-trekking experience. The plan was first to travel the 975 kilometers from the coast of Antarctica to the South Pole. This portion of the journey would be all uphill and against the wind. The last 1,500 kilometers – from the South Pole to the opposite coast – would be downhill and with the wind. The goal: to reach the other side of the Antarctic continent in time to catch a free ride home on a tourist cruise ship.

Team Member: So we started the wheels turning, of becoming an organization, working on our mission and our vision.

Narrator: Carrying out an enormous undertaking like this required months of planning, organizing, training, and fund-raising. Ann's background as a teacher led her to a creative solution for financing this expensive expedition. The team publicized the expedition in schools and received contributions from tens of thousands of schoolchildren and ordinary citizens – one dollar, five dollars, and ten dollars at a time. As the time for the expedition approached, the team gathered and packed the supplies and equipment they would need for almost four months on the ice.

• • •

Narrator: On October 30, they arrived in Punta Arenas, Chile. From there, it would be a ten-hour plane ride to Antarctica. But bad weather delayed their departure for nine days – days they would have to make up in order to meet their cruise ship for the trip home.

• • •

Narrator: Finally, the long-awaited day arrived.

Team Member: The plane ride – looking down out of the window – for me, was big, and seeing Antarctica and the mountains half-buried in ice.

Narrator: Day 1: Spirits were high. With this trip, they hoped to accomplish what no other women have ever done: to cross the Antarctic continent completely under their own power. All food and gear was set up for pairs. Changing tent mates every eight days would help relieve the stress of being in a small tent with the same person for four months. Pulling sleds of 110 kilos uphill and against the wind was demanding labor. To maintain their body weight, each woman had to consume 5,000 calories per day, forty-five percent of it from fat. Adding great quantities of butter to every pasta, rice, and meat dish helped provide the calories they needed. To keep on schedule, the team had to travel at least ten miles a day.

Team Member: Day 6: It was really discouraging today. We only came up with five miles.

Narrator: So they pushed even harder to make up the lost time, but the physical stress began to take its toll. In addition to sore, cramped muscles, Sunniva came down with a respiratory infection. Anne Dal-Vera developed painful tendinitis in her right foot. After thirty days of one thing or another, things went from bad to worse. Sunniva sprained her ankle.

(continued)

Sunniva Sorby: I couldn't fight anymore, because I found that not only did I not have anything left physically, I was fighting so hard I had nothing left here. And this scared me more than this scared me.

Narrator: Day 57: Morale was low. The team knew that Ann Bancroft, as the leader of the expedition, was considering radioing for an emergency evacuation of Sunniva by plane. Since all their equipment was set up for pairs, they wondered who else would have to leave with Sunniva. Because of her tendinitis, Anne Dal-Vera knew that second person would be her.

Anne Dal-Vera: It seemed to me that she had made the decision that I should go out.

Ann Bancroft: It wasn't an end-all decision at the time, but it was put very strongly towards her that "if Sunniva goes, you will probably have to go."

Narrator: Day 59: The dream of reaching their goal came alive again, if only briefly. A military supply plane flying to the South Pole dropped an unexpected package for the team.

Sunniva Sorby: We open it up and it says, "To the Antarctica explorers" – crossword puzzles, comic strips, homemade chocolate-chip cookies, four apples, and a rose.

Narrator: Some scientists and military personnel stationed on the coast of Antarctica had heard of the women's challenging expedition and had decided to send them a message of encouragement.

Sunniva Sorby: We were sort of sobbing – four very strong women who have skied, you know, over two months. It reminded me that I . . . I was still alive.

Narrator: The unexpected gift gave the team the mental strength they needed to continue.

Team Member: We could see the Pole for about a day of travel – about fourteen miles.

Narrator: With no roads or signs, Sue had managed to guide them accurately across the vast wasteland of Antarctica.

Ann Bancroft: We're seeing it . . . we're going there. At this point, I've got the group shoulder to shoulder because I want us to come in together to signify this team.

Narrator: The four women were able to reach the South Pole together without dogs, machines, or men. . . . But a difficult decision had to be made. Should Ann Bancroft and Sue Giller finish the journey by themselves?

Ann Bancroft: I was totally ready to go. Food was there. I'm in the best shape of my life.

Narrator: But the trip to the South Pole had taken longer than planned. If Ann and Sue didn't make it to the coast on time to meet the cruise ship, they would have to call for an expensive emergency evacuation. All four women decided to end their adventure together with their successful arrival at the South Pole.

Anne Dal-Vera: We all agreed. We felt that that was important: not to be the first all-women's expedition to be *rescued* from Antarctica.

Narrator: Several years have passed. Ann Bancroft still dreams of crossing the Antarctic continent.

Ann Bancroft: The demanding mental fortitude that it takes is really intriguing to me. You grow as a person as a result of . . . of those struggles.

Narrator: Today she is returning to Antarctica with a new partner, Liv Arnesen from Oslo, Norway. When this trip is over, Ann hopes she will have achieved the goal she was unable to accomplish on her first trip: to cross the entire Antarctic continent without dogs, machines, or men.

Author's Acknowledgments

A great number of people assisted in the development of the *New Interchange* Videos. Particular thanks go to the following:

The **students** and **teachers** in the following schools and institutes who pilot-tested the Videos or the Video Activity Books; their valuable comments and suggestions helped shape the content of the entire program:

Athenée Français, Tokyo, Japan; **Centro Cultural Brasil-Estados Unidos**, Belém, Brazil; **Eurocentres**, Virginia, U.S.A.; **Fairmont State College**, West Virginia, U.S.A.; **Hakodate Daigaku**, Hokkaido, Japan; **Hirosaki Gakuin Daigaku**, Aomori, Japan; **Hiroshima Shudo Daigaku**, Hiroshima, Japan; **Hokkaido Daigaku, Institute of Language and Cultural Studies**, Hokkaido, Japan; **The Institute Meguro**, Tokyo, Japan; **Instituto Brasil-Estados Unidos**, Rio de Janeiro, Brazil; **Instituto Cultural de Idiomas**, Caxias do Sul, Brazil; **Instituto Cultural Peruano-Norteamericano**, Lima, Peru; **Musashino Joshi Daigaku**, Tokyo, Japan; **Nagasaki Gaigo Tanki Daigaku**, Nagasaki, Japan; **New Cida**, Tokyo, Japan; **Parco-ILC English School**, Chiba, Japan; **Pegasus Language Services**, Tokyo, Japan; **Poole Gakuin Tanki Daigaku**, Hyogo, Japan; **Seinan Gakuin Daigaku**, Fukuoka, Japan; **Shukugawa Joshi Tanki Daigaku**, Hyogo, Japan; **Tokai Daigaku**, Kanagawa, Japan; **YMCA Business School**, Kanagawa, Japan; and **Yokohama YMCA**, Kanagawa, Japan.

The **editorial** and **production** team on *New Interchange* Video Level Three: Pam Bernstein, Sylvia P. Bloch, Patti Brecht, Karen Brock, Karen Davy, Hilary Grant, Pauline Ireland, Kathy Niemczyk, Jennifer O'Keeffe, Bill Paulk, Mary Sandre, Howard Siegelman, and Mary Vaughn.

And Cambridge University Press **staff** and **advisors**: Kanako Aoki, Carlos Barbisan, Kathleen Corley, Kate Cory-Wright, Riitta da Costa, Peter Davison, Peter Donovan, Cecilia Gómez, Colin Hayes, Koen Van Landeghem, Alex Martínez, Nigel McQuitty, Carine Mitchell, Andy Paz, Dan Schulte, Catherine Shih, Alcione Tavares, Su-Wei Wong, and Ellen Zlotnick.

And a special thanks to the video producer, Master Communications Group.